THE *American Foreign Policy*

THE AMERICAN IMAGE SERIES
Ernest R. May, General Editor

THE AMERICAN SOCIETY
Edited by Kenneth S. Lynn

THE AMERICAN FOREIGN POLICY
Edited by Ernest R. May

THE AMERICAN POLITICAL PROCESS
Edited by Leonard W. Levy and John P. Roche

THE AMERICAN ECONOMY
Edited by Jesse W. Markham

THE
American
Foreign
Policy

EDITED BY *Ernest R. May*

George Braziller   NEW YORK   1963

PREFACE

*I*N THE AUTUMN of 1961 Harvard University was asked to organize an orientation program for seventy-five Brazilian student leaders being sent to the United States by the Cultural Union of São Paulo and the Department of State. The Office of Latin American Studies at Harvard arranged for four of us, specialists in American studies, to work with these students during the ten days they were to be in Cambridge.

When we began to prepare the program, we discovered that there were no suitable texts either in Portuguese or English. Such books of readings as existed were designed for college courses or, at the very least, assumed some specialized knowledge on the part of the reader. While we could expect the Brazilian students to be intelligent and well-informed about Brazil, we had to assume that they would know almost nothing about how the United States had grown, what its culture was, or how its democracy or economic system worked. To meet their needs, we felt we should put together four entirely new volumes containing basic readings.

When the Brazilian students arrived, these volumes were not yet ready. The four of us circulated some of the readings among them. We also talked with them at length and tried to answer their questions and find out what about the United States interested and puzzled them.

We are not sure yet what effect our teaching may have had. Among those hostile to the United States, we did not look for conversion. What we hoped was merely that all of them would go home knowing more about America, unable any longer to voice oversimplifications, and to this extent we think we did succeed. In any event, we hope that these four volumes, with their introductions, will enable others to undertake similar ventures.

Unlike comparable works, these volumes are designed for readers who have no specialized background in these fields, and, because they were constructed with a foreign audience in mind, they introduce perspectives that may be interesting even to specialists. While foreign readers should find in them the profile of America, readers nearer home may get, as well, a sense of the American image.

ERNEST R. MAY

CONTENTS

I. Colonial Area

The Objects of Revolution

The Declaration of Independence   29

II. Neutralist State

Alliance with Revolutionary France

Washington's Farewell Address   48

III. Leader of a Neutral Bloc

America's Mission in the Hemisphere

The Monroe Doctrine   68

IV. Have-Not Nation

The Merits of the Mexican War

V. Nation Beset by Civil Strife

The Issues of the Civil War

VI. Colonial Power

VII. Missionary State: First Phase

VIII. Missionary State: Second Phase

IX. Super-Power

X. Perspectives of the Sixties

INTRODUCTION

Ernest R. May

$\mathcal{M}$ANY PEOPLE in other parts of the world look on the United States as a gigantic adolescent—a nation immensely strong but lacking tact, discretion, prudence, wisdom, and experience. Partly because they try so hard to see themselves as others see them, many Americans accept this image as a true one.

A few years ago I sat on a panel with Charles M. Drury, a former Deputy Minister of National Defence in the Canadian government. His subject was Canadian-American relations, and it surprised me to hear him conclude, "In the larger sphere we are indeed fortunate to be alongside as beneficent, as powerful, and as wise . . . a country as the United States."

The unexpected word was "wise." It is not a term often applied to the United States, even by Americans.

Yet this ought not to be so, at least not if there is any relation between wisdom and experience, for Americans are in some ways the most experienced people taking part in world politics.

Less than two hundred years ago, their land was a colonial area. It went through a revolution for independence. Afterward it was a new, small nation trying to survive in a world torn by the rivalry of two great powers, England and France. The policy it adopted was neutralism.

When France was beaten, a polite cold war developed between Britain and Tsarist Russia, and meanwhile the Spanish empire in the Americas splintered. The United States took advantage of this situation to proclaim the Monroe Doctrine and thus become leader of what today would be called a neutral bloc or third force.

Becoming bigger and stronger, the United States demanded and got from Britain part of Oregon and made war on Mexico to take land from her. It was a dissatisfied nation, a disturber of the *status quo*. It could have been called a "have-not" nation. (It was not such, but neither were the have-not powers of the 1930's, Italy, Japan, and

Germany.) The modern counterparts are Nasser's Egypt, perhaps even Communist China.

The American Civil War was unique in that it came so long after independence, involved such large and well-disciplined forces, and turned on a clear moral issue, slavery. Otherwise it resembled the civil strife that seems to wrack most new states, testing whether they are nations or not and exposing them to the temptation and peril of outside intervention. (One of the more startling parallels that can be drawn is between Jefferson Davis, the President of the Southern Confederacy, and Mr. Moise Tshombe, the leader of the Congo separatists.)

By the end of the nineteenth century, rapid industrial growth had made the United States a great power. In 1898 it went to war with Spain—not this time for territorial gain but rather because the people could not contain their sympathy for a Cuban revolution for independence. As an almost accidental result, it emerged as the possessor of Puerto Rico and the Philippines. It thus became for a time a colonial power.

In the first and second world wars, the United States intervened belatedly on the Allied side. Both times its professed goals were to reform international relations, end wars forever, and spread American-style democracy, the rule of law, and what went with it, to all peoples on the globe. It was then a missionary power, preaching its gospel unto all parts much as (though not in the same ways as) the Communist U.S.S.R.

Since World War II it has been a super-power, living with the knowledge that its action or inaction could cause a catastrophe for the world. Among all nations in the parade of history, only the present-day Soviet Union has known similar responsibility.

This is an extraordinary range of experience.

Including just about every condition that can be found in the modern world, it should give Americans a unique capacity for understanding other peoples and most Americans would claim that it does. President Eisenhower cited the past as the reason Americans could not really resent neutralism. During one of his press conferences he remarked, "We were a young country once, and our whole policy for the first 150 years was, we were neutral." Similarly, President Kennedy declared in his speech to the U.N., "My nation was once a colony, and we know what colonialism means."

Others do not necessarily respect these claims. An Asian or African may rejoin that most European states were once colonies of Rome without that fact having had any appreciable effect on their attitudes toward subject peoples. He could add that only a fraction of the American population knows what it is like to be colored in a white man's world.

But while there is some substance in such objections, there is also some in the American claims. Memories of the past are more real and important to Americans than most Asians or Africans or Europeans think—more so, indeed, than many Americans realize.

In the first place, the experience of being colonists and makers of a new nation is relatively recent, and it has retained a relevance that ancient history does not have for any Europeans except the Greeks. In the Civil War Confederates appealed to revolutionary precedents. So did Southerners and Westerners supporting William Jennings Bryan for the presidency in 1896 and protesting the tyranny of the Northeast. So as recently as the 1930's did various writers, including Walter Prescott Webb in his eloquent *Divided We Stand*, contending that the South and West still occupied a colonial status. Whether actual similarities existed or not, people thought they did, and the fact illustrates how fresh in mind such memories remained.

In the second place, it is arguable that Americans draw on their historical experience when judging foreign affairs because it is the chief resource they have.

The reasons lie in several paradoxes.

One is that American history is unusually important to Americans because so many of them are not of American origin. Even though legislation of the 1920's curbed immigration, as late as 1950 one-quarter of the population was still foreign-born or of foreign-born parentage. At least two-thirds of the people have ancestors who came to the country less than a hundred years ago. Only a tiny minority can claim descent on both sides from families that were in the United States at the time of the revolution.

Each wave of immigrants had to learn American traditions. Cherishing what they had, the older settlers were always fearful lest newcomers change or spoil it. For that reason, tests on American history and government were required for naturalization. Partly for that reason, the majority of states emphasized these subjects in their schools, some even making them mandatory in universities.

A survey of typical school systems in the 1940's found all requiring five to seven years of American history. None demanded more than two years of "world history"; some offered nothing but a course on "The European Background of United States History." As a result, every American has learned something of his country's past.

In England a workman stopped on a street would probably not be able to identify many of the prime ministers since 1783 or to say how British constitutional issues are decided. In the United States almost any literate citizen can name a third of the thirty-five presidents and state at least generally the functions of the Supreme Court. The average American has an unusual amount of academic knowledge about his nation.

This has not been entirely forced. Many immigrants wanted to learn about the new land. To compete economically and socially with people already there, they had to copy their ways. In the process some of the sons and grandsons of immigrants became more American than the earlier Americans.

In some of the great debates on foreign policy, as in that between Woodrow Wilson and Henry Cabot Lodge over entry into the League of Nations, immigrant groups were mostly to be found on the traditionalist side. Some in the 1950's were fervent in support of the spurious "Americanism" of Senator Joseph R. McCarthy. This was true especially of Polish-Americans and Irish-Americans. Others, however, notably in the predominantly immigrant American Jewish

Congress, saw more quickly than most how the McCarthy movement threatened traditional liberties, while the Daughters of the American Revolution did not.

The point is that memories of the American past, whether clouded or clear, have been drilled into Americans and have been important to them because so many are of immigrant background.

A second paradox is that while Americans are relatively well-educated and well-read, they know very little about any country but their own. The schools' emphasis on American studies is partly responsible. While an English workingman might know less about his country than an American about his, an English university graduate or professional man would be much more likely than an American to know something about the history of Asia, Africa, and even South America.

Travel does not fill the void. Americans are a highly mobile people; one person in five moves every year; yet few ever get outside the continental limits. Except for those with overseas military service, probably not more than four per cent of the population has ever seen Europe, Asia, Africa, or Latin America.

Nor do reading, radio-listening, and television-watching take the place of education and travel. Although there are in the United States over 1,700 daily newspapers, 8,000 weeklies, 3,000 magazines, and countless newscasts, only a handful of dailies and a half-dozen or so weekly broadcasts give more than cursory attention to foreign happenings other than crises.

Traditionally Americans have had little interest in other lands. Undoubtedly one reason is again the immigrant background of so much of the population. In the second generation, the passion for Americanization was often accompanied by rejection of all that smacked of the old country. In many cases, this was the form that adolescent rebellion took in immigrant families.

Another reason is that political and economic life in America is so fragmented. Such questions as the paving of streets, the laying of sewage lines, and the building of schools are decided in the locality.

The police are there. Corruption is mainly there rather than in the national or even the state capital. Prices, sales, rates of interest, and job opportunities are largely matters of the local market. Even in regard to national issues such as income tax rates, the point of pressure is in the locality—on the Congressman who lives there.

For Americans, knowledge of world and even national affairs has traditionally been academic. It has not seemed relevant to everyday life in the way that it is for peoples with more centralized governments and livelihoods more directly affected by foreign markets. Not given such knowledge in school, Americans have not acquired it, and when forced by circumstances to form opinions about foreign lands or issues of foreign policy they have been driven back upon the knowledge they do have—that of their own country's past.

A third paradox is that, in spite of the variety of conditions that are part of this past, Americans feel inexperienced in international affairs. From time immemorial they have thought of themselves as ingenuous and of all foreigners as wily. The stereotype images are counterparts to the country bumpkin and the city slicker.

These feelings have had some foundation. For a century and a half the nation was isolated from world politics (which during those years were chiefly European politics). Not until World War II did most people concede that events on the other half of the globe should concern them. Only after seeing nuclear weapons and long-range missiles in the hands of the Russians did any number realize that such concern might no longer be a matter of choice.

By tradition the country had had complete freedom of will. Men debated intervention in the two world wars and participation in the League and the United Nations on the assumption that the issue was what *should* be done, not what *had* to be done. Almost everyone supposed that the nation could do whatever it wanted to.

Even the questions of joining the North Atlantic Pact and intervening in Korea were argued in this way. But by that time there had already grown up an uneasy fear that the future might bring occasions when a full range of alternatives would not be open. Increasingly it became apparent to Americans that not only could they be seriously affected by what another government or people did but that their decisions and moves might not control events.

This was a startling and unsettling realization. Some of those who followed McCarthy and his imitators were taking refuge in the fantasy that the new predicament could be blamed on alien, subversive influences within the United States itself. Others fled to the belief that if the American government would only put away its arms and go back to acting as it had in the past, the predicament would go away.

The majority found it hard to accept such diagnoses. Since the early 1950's the emphasis in speech and writing has been on the newness of the situation. The lessons preached over and over by statesmen and commentators are that the danger of utter destruction exists and will not end, that circumstances will arise requiring action of some kind and offering choices not between good and bad but between evils, that there is little hope of a future better than the present, and that the United States may have to strain its resources and wits merely to prevent its situation from becoming worse.

For such conditions Americans feel poorly equipped. There is among them an almost universal sense of self-reproach, even shame, about failure to take a larger part in world affairs in the past. Refusal to enter the League of Nations is now regarded as irresponsible. The popular isolationism of the 1920's and 1930's is looked back upon as evidence of national immaturity. So, to some extent, is the optimism of World War II.

And this is the final paradox—that, finding their historical experience insufficient preparation for new conditions, they search for better comprehension by rooting more deeply into that experience.

While sales of books do not necessarily mean anything, it may be significant that the best-seller lists of the decade after 1950 included an unusual number of serious historical works—George F. Kennan's *American Diplomacy, 1900-1950,* Frederick Lewis Allen's *The Big Change,* former President Truman's *Memoirs,* then-Senator John F. Kennedy's *Profiles in Courage,* Allan Nevins's studies on the Civil

War era, and the volumes by Arthur M. Schlesinger, Jr., on the age
of Franklin D. Roosevelt.

More significant evidence is in the words of leaders who were
speaking to and for the public. Leafing through the addresses and
messages of Truman, Eisenhower, and Kennedy and the transcribed
speeches of Adlai Stevenson and Richard Nixon, one cannot help
being struck by the frequency with which they all cite episodes in
American history as parallels for events and conditions abroad. The
past of their own nation is of necessity the chief source from which
Americans derive attitudes toward other lands and ideas about the
policies that their government should follow.

A few years hence this may not be so true. Owing partly to decline
in the proportion of foreign-born, pressure on schools to stress
"Americanism" has dwindled. Organizations continuing loudly to
advocate it, such as the American Legion, consist largely of men in
late middle age. Parent-Teacher Associations representing younger
generations agitate for broadening the curricula. The trend is now
toward an increase in the amount of teaching about other peoples and
cultures.

Although the newsprint and broadcast time given to international
affairs is still relatively meager, the proportion steadily grows. The
daily with the best foreign coverage, the *New York Times,* has had
mounting national circulation. Weekly news digests such as *Time* and
Newsweek not only keep gaining readers but give more space to
foreign events than in the past. There has even been increased demand for imported journals such as *The Economist* and *The
Observer.*

In addition to works on American history, the best-seller lists of
the 1950's and 1960's included Arnold Toynbee's *Study of History,*
Churchill's volumes on World War II, Kennan's later book, *Russia
and the West under Lenin and Stalin,* and, as one of the more spectacular sales successes, William L. Shirer's *Rise and Fall of the Third
Reich.*

Such signs indicate that Americans seek to know more about the actual experiences and conditions of other peoples. It may be that by the 1970's their attitudes and ideas will have new and broader foundations. For the present, however, one who wishes insight into American perspective must look at the American past. That is where the guidelines are still to be found.

The selections that follow include documents that have been touchstones for American attitudes and policies: the Declaration of Independence, Washington's Farewell Address, the Monroe Doctrine, the Open Door notes, and the Preamble to the Charter of the United Nations organization.

At one time or another each of the first four has been looked upon almost as holy writ. The Declaration of Independence still is. Although the Farewell Address lost some of its sanctity with the decline of isolationism, parts of it are still quoted with reverence. So is the Monroe Doctrine, even though it has virtually been abrogated by treaties obliging the United States to accept majority rule within the Organization of American States. So are the Open Door notes, at least in some circles, despite the fact that historical research can locate almost no instance in which the policy was ever enforced and that whatever meaning it had was lost when China turned Communist.

The Preamble to the U.N. Charter has a different status. It lacks the mystique. On the other hand, it has been cited by every Secretary of State since 1945 as the fundamental statement of American policy objectives.

These five texts are basic. To borrow the Book of Common Prayer's assertion about the first two commandments: on them hang all the law and the prophets.

The other documents show the dialogues from which these texts emerged and also the debates that have taken place at crucial moments in the American past.

Most are from Presidents or at least from men who were major party nominees for the presidency. Aside from the first two, which date from before the Revolution, the exceptions are those from

Hamilton, Lodge, Wallace, and Taft. But Hamilton was the fore-most man in his party. At a time when the constitutional system was new, he served as virtual prime minister under Washington. Lodge, long a leader in the Senate, was his party's spokesman on foreign affairs. Wallace served as Vice-President and, but for accidents of time and politics, might have been Roosevelt's successor. At the time when he started to criticize the Truman policies he was still widely mentioned as a possible Democratic nominee. Taft, like Lodge, was a leader in the Senate and in every election year from 1940 to 1952 had strong support for the Republican nomination. All were respon-sible leaders of large bodies of public opinion. With the possible exception of Lincoln in 1848 and Jefferson Davis in the 1860's, all spoke in hope or expectation that a majority of the people would agree with what they said.

These documents therefore illustrate something else about the American experience besides its variety. They indicate the extent to which each past change has involved serious public debate. Issues and alternatives were put before the people not just by journalists and agitators but by responsible men. More often than not they were men hoping to win election or re-election as President.

In recent years almost nothing has caused Americans such concern as the absence of debate on foreign policy. In their two election con-tests, Eisenhower and Stevenson found little to disagree about in this area except the timing of a moratorium on nuclear tests. While Ken-nedy and Nixon appeared to quarrel in 1960 about Cuba and Quemoy and Matsu, by the time they had clarified their positions the differ-ences could have been detected only by a Jesuit.

Almost no one has uncovered a clear issue. Yet every national leader, including all recent presidents and presidential candidates, Congressional captains, and business and labor spokesmen, expresses real alarm at the lack of debate. The saw, "there are two sides to every question," is an article of faith, and apprehension develops when only one side can be seen.

This faith also affects American attitudes toward other countries.

To the question of why Fascism or Communism is so repugnant, the inevitable answer is that such a system denies people freedom. If asked to be more specific, some Americans might mention religious or economic freedom first. Most, however, would start with freedom of expression—the opportunity for dissent to be heard. This would be the reply even of someone, such as a Daughter of the American Revolution, who in practice was not particularly tolerant of dissent at home.

Nothing can so quickly stir ill-feeling in Americans as evidence that another government is suppressing debate. Generalissimo Chiang Kai-shek's popularity has weathered much. Prewar and wartime propaganda fixed the image of him as an oriental Abraham Lincoln, and most subsequent revelations failed to cause a change. But even he lost standing when it was reported in September, 1960, that he had imprisoned Lei Chen and closed down the only opposition journal on Taiwan. At any rate, some newspapers, including the editorially cautious *New York Times*, attacked his regime as a dictatorship.

Conversely, nothing causes a favorable change in American views more quickly than evidence that a repressive state is lifting bans on debate. Each time that Moscow or Peiping announces some step toward freer speech, the result is a flood of hopeful commentary.

This fact points to one of the assumptions underlying faith in free debate. Americans expect it to yield consensus or at least compromise.

Their own experience does not necessarily justify this opinion. The Revolution was not stopped by talk. War with England came in 1812 in spite of nine years of negotiation. The Civil War was not prevented by debates in Congress over slavery and other sectional issues. But, as Americans understand this experience, it does not negate their theory.

The popular interpretation of the Revolution has always been that the British crown was to blame for failing to heed American protests and make concessions. Of the war of 1812 it is universally believed that it could have been avoided if negotiation had only continued for a few more weeks. And with regard to the Civil War, a widely held view, at least in recent decades, has been that it was needless,

that compromises could have been effected, slavery abolished gradually, and the union preserved by discussion rather than force.

So soon after World War II it is still the general opinion that
Hitler was a madman with whom no concord was possible. But a
number of historians have charged that Roosevelt brought on the
Pearl Harbor attack by refusing to negotiate seriously with the
Japanese about a compromise on China. This interpretation has found
its way into many of the texts used in schools. If the past is any guide,
it seems probable that Americans will someday regard the war started
by Hitler in 1939 as one that could have been prevented by more
discussion, debate, and negotiation.

The Soviet Union has perplexed and alarmed Americans because
it has been so hard to deal with. From their standpoint it seems that
Franklin Roosevelt offered every possible concession but that the
Russians made no attempt to meet him even part way. In 1946, Stalin
was invited to approve the Acheson-Lilienthal plan, by which the
United States would strip itself of nuclear weapons, turn over to a
U.N. agency all its facilities for making atomic bombs, and agree to
an absolute ban on their future manufacture. The only reservations
made by the American government were that the timing be such as to
insure American safety during the change-over and that enforcement
of the ban be not subject to a veto in the U.N. Security Council.
Although the Russians then had no workable atomic bombs, Stalin
rejected these plans.

Americans were totally unable to comprehend his action. To most
the only interpretation that seemed credible was that the Soviet government simply wanted no agreement—that its object was to create
tension and antagonism.

For a time after Stalin's death there was some inclination to believe
that, like Hitler, he had been beyond the reach of reason. Americans
talked of a thaw in the cold war. But when first Malenkov and then
Khrushchev proved equally intractable, they were thrown again into
incomprehension. The common view is summed up in Churchill's
phrase: the Russians are "a mystery wrapped in an enigma."

Such hopes as Americans still have reside in the belief that gradual freeing of debate within the U.S.S.R. will bring changes in the positions of its government. It is almost impossible for them to believe that between reasonable men there can be conflicts of opinion or will that cannot sooner or later be solved by talk.

One reason for this ingrained attitude is evident in these selections. Here are extracts from some of the great debates on foreign policy. Because in the United States external and internal affairs have never been separable, they touch on many great domestic issues. Yet any reader must be struck by the extent to which the antagonists, Hamilton and Jefferson, Lincoln and Polk, Bryan and Theodore Roosevelt, Wilson and Lodge, Hoover and Franklin Roosevelt, and Wallace, Truman, and Taft, are in fundamental agreement. They all appeal to the same traditions and moral standards. Except as between Lincoln and Jefferson Davis, one can almost say that none differed about objectives.

Louis Hartz has pointed out in his brilliant book, *The Liberal Tradition in America,* that the nation never had for any long period either a feudal caste or an entrammeled proletariat and hence never had significant factions fighting either to preserve hereditary privileges or to batter them down. Consequently, Americans never even witnessed such implacable hostilities as those that existed in Europe between arch-conservatives and Socialists and Communists.

The men whose verbal battles are illustrated here were all in agreement about the kind of society they wanted. All accepted the principle of human equality. (This was true even of Davis; he simply denied that Negroes were humans.) They were all in accord that the individual should enjoy maximum freedom. And while it is the case that Americans expect and desire free debate within and between nations, it has to be remembered that this is the kind of debate they have in mind—one in which means to ends are at issue, not ends themselves.

The inability of Americans to imagine that there are insoluble issues is thus due in part to their immersion in their own history. Nor is this the only handicap they suffer from that cause.

While their past includes a wide variety of conditions, in each instance their experience has been in some way limited. Memories of the colonial era, for example, are chiefly those pertaining to Englishmen who lived in an English colony in the eighteenth century.

After President Kennedy had said in his U.N. speech that Americans could understand colonial peoples because of their own colonial background, he went on to observe that among the colonial areas of the present day were the Soviet satellite states in Eastern Europe. In part, undoubtedly, he meant this remark as a goad to the Asian and African leaders who had recently met at Belgrade, passed resolutions attacking Western colonialism, but omitted to say anything reproachful against the Communist powers. It was more than a clever argument, however; it was intended seriously. And it is quite significant, for it suggests what President Kennedy and the majority of Americans understand to be the chief problem of colonial people.

It is the same as that of English colonists in America—the absence of self-government. The President was saying that historical experience enables Americans to understand a people's objecting to laws or ordinances they had no part in framing, governors they did not help to choose, and economic restrictions that limit their commerce or economic development in the interest of some other land.

There are, however, situations to which the American experience is not relevant. The independence movement in the Union of South Africa had entirely different motivations. Mr. Tshombe's Katangese resisted rule by the central government of the Congo because they wanted to remain under Belgian domination. In the various uprisings in Eastern Europe, including that in Hungary in 1956, it is regrettably the case that substantial numbers sided with the Russians. (As a matter of fact, a substantial number of Americans sided with the British in 1776. The proportion may have been as much as a third. But theirs is a position that the American memory has practically suppressed. One has to go to a rare book depository even to find facsimiles of their pamphlets.)

In general, Americans have to deal with these situations by rationalizing them out of existence. Thus most commentary on South Africa stresses the minority in that country that agitates for an end to racist legislation. Most journalists treated Tshombe as a puppet and assumed that he did not have the backing of his people. Even the curious troupe of right-wingers defending him felt obliged to pretend that he had no ties with Belgians, speaking of his forces as "freedom fighters." And one must look in very specialized works by scholars to discover any data about partisans of Russia in Eastern Europe.

The most striking case in which Americans have shown inability to understand situations outside their own experience is that of Cuba. When Castro's revolution first succeeded, the huge majority of Americans were sympathetic. His seemed the kind of movement they understood—one directed against a tyranny, professing desire for greater democracy, liberty, and economic freedom.

Contrary to the general impression abroad, American public opinion was not alienated by seizures of American property. Desire for freedom from foreign domination, even domination by American capital, was comprehensible. Nor was there sharp reaction even to the first overtures made by Castro to the Soviet Union. Many people saw in these merely evidence that Cuba might flirt with neutralism, and this, too, was understandable.

The violent turn came when Americans realized that Cuba was going farther, that it would actually align itself with the Soviets and Chinese, and that it would soon be a Communist state. This seemed incredible. It was beyond American comprehension that any people could voluntarily accept satellite status, abandon democracy and political liberty, and surrender to regimentation and dictatorship.

As was demonstrated by the events leading to the Bay of Pigs landing, highly placed and very well-informed Americans remained unable to credit the facts. They assumed that the Cuban populace must somehow have been tricked and that they would overthrow Castro if given a chance. As the landing proved, this was a delusion. Through such shock therapy, most people in the government were cured; the majority of Americans were not, and probably could not be. Limited largely to what they drew from their own historical experience, they had nothing to assist their understanding. At best they could only view Cuba, like Russia, as a mystery.

It remains a fact that American experience has been diverse. It is also a fact that Americans know their history well and that, as a result, they have greater capacity than any people in the world for understanding the variety of conditions in which other men live. The selections in this volume illustrate not only through how many phases the United States has passed but also how rich and vigorous was the debate at each turn. They suggest the insights that Americans have taken from their history and the many still to be found there. At the same time, they also indicate what the American past has not had—prolonged conflicts over fundamentals, issues that did not seem soluble by debate, and situations in which substantial numbers had aspirations other than those summed up in the Declaration of Independence.

American readers are apt to find the title of this volume odd. Unlike Frenchmen or Spaniards, used to hearing of *le politique extérieur* or *la política exterior,* they are unaccustomed to seeing "foreign policy" with a definite article. Yet in many ways this form is more appropriate than any other and more appropriate for the United States than any other nation, at least at present. Although policy is a vague word, the simplest definition for it is "means to an end." Not differing significantly about national goals, Americans through their first century and a half debated what means to employ. But, as is suggested in more detail in the notes accompanying the documents, what had happened by the 1950's was that the historic alternatives had become merged. Americans found themselves not only with one set of objectives but, broadly speaking, with only one method of moving there—one foreign policy. What that policy is and how it developed, the documents attempt to show.

I.   Colonial Area

The American Revolution was not at the outset a revolution for independence. Although a state of war developed, after the clashes of arms at Lexington and Concord in April, 1775, American leaders insisted that they were Englishmen contending for English rights against a king who had exceeded his powers—much as Englishmen had done in England in the seventeenth century. Only as time passed did sentiment grow for an outright break with the mother country. Not until the summer of 1776 did a majority in the colonial Continental Congress come around to this view.

The intervening year saw one of the formative debates in American history—that between men viewing the colonies as inseparably linked with England and Europe and others holding that North America had an identity and destiny all its own. The eminent lawyer and pamphleteer, John Dickinson, of Pennsylvania, though an early leader in the protest movement, belonged to the former group. Tom Paine, onetime sailor, corsetmaker, beggar, and tax collector, a chronic controversialist, and a newcomer to the colonies, was the most eloquent spokesman for the second group. Widely read and discussed, his tract Common Sense *has been credited by some historians with producing the decision for independence.*

Although Dickinson and Paine were opponents, one cannot help

*being struck by similarities in their arguments, especially in the values
to which they appealed. Their exchange illustrates the moral consensus that had already developed in America. The Declaration of
Independence is its classic statement.*

JOHN DICKINSON AND

TOM PAINE ON

THE OBJECTS OF REVOLUTION

We are reduced to the alternative of choosing an unconditional sub-mission to the tyranny of irritated ministers, or resistance by force. The latter is our choice. —JOHN DICKINSON, 1775.

OUR FOREFATHERS, inhabitants of the island of Great Britain, left their native land, to seek on these shores a residence for civil and religious freedom. At the expence of their blood, at the hazard of their fortunes, without the least charge to the country from which they removed, by unceasing labour and an unconquerable spirit, they effected settlements in the distant and inhospitable wilds of America, then filled with numerous and warlike nations of barbarians. Societies or governments, vested with perfect legislatures, were formed under charters from the crown, and an harmonious intercourse was estab-lished between the colonies and the kingdom from which they de-rived their origin. The mutual benefits of this union became in a short time so extraordinary, as to excite astonishment. It is univer-sally confessed, that the amazing increase of the wealth, strength, and navigation of the realm, arose from this source; and the minister,

Declaration by the Representatives of the United Colonies of North America, setting forth the causes and necessity of their taking up arms, July 6, 1775. *The Political Writings of John Dickinson, Esquire.* Wilmington, Del., 1801, vol. I, pp. 32-43.

who so wisely and successfully directed the measures of Great Britain in the late war, publicly declared, that these colonies enabled her to triumph over her enemies. Towards the conclusion of that war, it pleased our sovereign to make a change in his counsels. From that fatal moment, the affairs of the British empire began to fall into confusion. . . . The new ministry finding the brave foes of Britain, though frequently defeated, yet still contending, took up the unfortunate idea of granting them a hasty peace, and of then subduing her faithful friends.

These devoted colonies were judged to be in such a state, as to present victories without bloodshed, and all the easy emoluments of statuteable plunder. The uninterrupted tenor of their peaceable and respectful behaviour from the beginning of colonization, their dutiful, zealous, and useful services during the war . . . could not save them from the meditated innovations. . . .

Administration sensible that we should regard these oppressive measures as freemen ought to do, sent over fleets and armies to inforce them. The indignation of the Americans was roused, it is true; but it was the indignation of a virtuous, loyal, and affectionate people. . . . We have pursued every temperate, every respectful measure. . . .; but subsequent events have shewn, how vain was this hope of finding moderation in our enemies. . . .

In brief, a part of these colonies now feel, and all of them are sure of feeling, as far as the vengeance of administration can inflict them, the complicated calamities of fire, sword, and famine. We are reduced to the alternative of choosing an unconditional submission to the tyranny of irritated ministers, or resistance by force. The latter is our choice. WE HAVE COUNTED THE COST OF THIS CONTEST, AND FIND NOTHING SO DREADFUL AS VOLUNTARY SLAVERY. Honour, justice, and humanity, forbid us tamely to surrender that freedom which we received from our gallant ancestors, and which our innocent posterity have a right to receive from us. We cannot endure the infamy and guilt of resigning succeeding generations to that wretchedness which inevitably awaits them, if we basely entail hereditary bondage upon them.

Our cause is just. Our union is perfect. Our internal resources are great, and, if necessary, foreign assistance is undoubtedly attainable. We gratefully acknowledge, as signal instances of the Divine favour towards us, that His providence would not permit us to be called into this severe controversy, until we were grown up to our present strength, had been previously exercised in warlike operations, and possessed the means of defending ourselves. With hearts fortified by these animating reflections, we most solemnly, before God and the world, DECLARE, that, exerting the utmost energy of those powers, which our beneficent Creator hath graciously bestowed upon us, the arms we have been compelled by our enemies to assume, we will, in defiance of every hazard, with unabating firmness and persever-ence, employ for the preservation of our liberties; being with one mind resolved to die freemen rather than to live slaves.

Lest this declaration should disquiet the minds of our friends and fellow-subjects in any part of the empire, we assure them that we mean not to dissolve that union which has so long and so happily subsisted between us, and which we sincerely wish to see restored. Necessity has not yet driven us into that desperate measure, or in-duced us to excite any other nation to war against them. We have not raised armies with ambitious designs of separating them from Great Britain and establishing independent states. We fight not for glory or for conquest. We exhibit to mankind the remarkable spectacle of a people attacked by unprovoked enemies, without any imputation or even suspicion of offence. . . .

In our own native land, in defence of the freedom that is our birth-right, and which we ever enjoyed till the late violation of it— for the protection of our property, acquired solely by the honest in-dustry of our fore-fathers and ourselves, against violence actually offered, we have taken up arms. We shall lay them down when hostilities shall cease on the part of the aggressors, and all danger of their being renewed shall be removed, and not before.

'Tis not the affair of a City, a County, a Province, or a Kingdom; but of a Continent—of at least one-eighth part of the habitable Globe. 'Tis not the concern of a day, a year, or an age; posterity are virtually involved in the contest. . . . Now is the seed-time of continental union, faith and honour.   —TOM PAINE, 1775.

*I*N THE FOLLOWING pages I offer nothing more than simple facts, plain arguments, and common sense: and have no other preliminaries to settle with the reader, than that he will divest himself of prejudice and prepossession, and suffer his reason and his feelings to determine for themselves: that he will put on, or rather that he will not put off, the true character of a man, and generously enlarge his views beyond the present day.

Volumes have been written on the subject of the struggle between England and America. Men of all ranks have embarked in the controversy, from different motives, and with various designs; but all have been ineffectual, and the period of debate is closed. Arms as the last resource decide the contest; the appeal was the choice of the King, and the Continent has accepted the challenge. . . .

The Sun never shined on a cause of greater worth. 'Tis not the affair of a City, a County, a Province, or a Kingdom; but of a Continent—of at least one-eighth part of the habitable Globe. 'Tis not the concern of a day, a year, or an age; posterity are virtually involved in the contest, and will be more or less affected even to the end of time, by the proceedings now. Now is the seed-time of Continental union, faith and honour. The least fracture now will be like a name engraved with the point of a pin on the tender rind of a young oak;

Thoughts on the Present State of American Affairs (1775), from Thomas Paine, *Common Sense Written by an Englishman.* Philadelphia, 1776.

the wound would enlarge with the tree, and posterity read in it full grown characters.

By referring the matter from argument to arms, a new era for politics is struck—a new method of thinking hath arisen. All plans, proposals, &c. prior . . . to the commencement of hostilities, are like the almanacks of the last year; which tho' proper then, are superceded and useless now. Whatever was advanced by the advocates on either side of the question then, terminated in one and the same point, *viz.* a union with Great Britain; the only difference between the parties was the method of effecting it; the one proposing force, the other friendship; but it hath so far happened that the first hath failed, and the second hath withdrawn her influence.

As much hath been said of the advantages of reconciliation, which, like an agreeable dream, hath passed away and left us as we were, it is but right that we should examine the contrary side of the argument, and enquire into some of the many material injuries which these Colonies sustain, and always will sustain, by being connected with and dependant on Great Britain. To examine that connection and dependance, on the principles of nature and common sense, to see what we have to trust to, if separated, and what we are to expect, if dependant.

I have heard it asserted by some, that as America has flourished under her former connection with Great Britain, the same connection is necessary towards her future happiness, and will always have the same effect. Nothing can be more fallacious than this kind of argument. We may as well assert that because a child has thrived upon milk, that it is never to have meat, or that the first twenty years of our lives is to become a precedent for the next twenty. But even this is admitting more than is true; for I answer roundly that America would have flourished as much and probably much more, had no European power taken any notice of her. The commerce by which she hath enriched herself are the necessaries of life, and will always have a market while eating is the custom of Europe.

But she has protected us, say some. That she hath engrossed us is true, and defended the Continent at our expense as well as her own, is admitted; and she would have defended Turkey from the same motive, *viz.* for the sake of trade and dominion.

Alas! we have been long led away by ancient prejudices and made large sacrifices to superstition. We have boasted the protection of Great Britain, without considering, that her motive was *interest* not *attachment;* and that she did not protect us from *our enemies* on *our account*: but from *her enemies* on *her own account,* from those who had no quarrel with us on any *other account,* and who will always be our enemies on the *same account.* Let Britain waive her pretensions to the Continent, or the Continent throw off the dependance, and we should be at peace with France and Spain, were they at war with Britain. . . . France and Spain never were, nor perhaps ever will be, our enemies as *Americans,* but as our being the *subjects of Great Britain.*

But Britain is the parent country, say some. Then the more shame upon her conduct. Even brutes do not devour their young, nor savages make war upon their families. Wherefore, the assertion, if true, turns to her reproach; but it happens not to be true, or only partly so, and the phrase *parent or mother country* hath been jesuitically adopted by the King and his parasites, with a low papistical design of gaining an unfair bias on the credulous weakness of our minds. Europe, and not England, is the parent country of America. This new World hath been the asylum for the persecuted lovers of civil and religious liberty from *every part* of Europe. Hither have they fled, not from the tender embraces of the mother, but from the cruelty of the monster; and it is so far true of England, that the same tyranny which drove the first emigrants from home, pursues their descendants still.

In this extensive quarter of the globe, we forget the narrow limits of three hundred and sixty miles (the extent of England) and carry our friendship on a larger scale; we claim brotherhood with every

European Christian, and triumph in the generosity of the sentiment.

It is pleasant to observe by what regular gradations we surmount the force of local prejudices, as we enlarge our acquaintance with the World. A man born in any town in England divided into parishes, will naturally associate most with his fellow parishioners (because their interests in many cases will be common) and distinguish him by the name of *neighbour*; if he meet him but a few miles from home, he drops the narrow idea of a street, and salutes him by the name of *townsman*; if he travel out of the county and meet him in any other, he forgets the minor divisions of street and town, and calls him *countryman*, *i.e. countyman*; but if in their foreign excursions they should associate in France, or any other part of *Europe*, their local remembrance would be enlarged into that of *Englishmen*. And by a just parity of reasoning, all Europeans meeting in America, or any other quarter of the globe, are *countrymen*; for England, Holland, Germany, or Sweden, when compared with the whole, stand in the same places on the larger scale, which the divisions of street, town, and county do on the smaller ones; Distinctions too limited for Continental minds. Not one third of the inhabitants, even of this province [Pennsylvania], are of English descent. Wherefore, I reprobate the phrase of Parent or Mother Country applied to England only, as being false, selfish, narrow and ungenerous.

But, admitting that we were all of English descent, what does it amount to? Nothing. Britain, being now an open enemy, extinguishes every other name and title: and to say that reconciliation is our duty, is truly farcical. The first king of England, of the present line [William the Conqueror] was a Frenchman, and half the peers of England are descendants from the same country; wherefore, by the same method of reasoning, England ought to be governed by France.

Much hath been said of the united strength of Britain and the Colonies, that in conjunction they might bid defiance to the world. But this is mere presumption; the fate of war is uncertain, neither do the expressions mean anything; for this continent would never suffer itself to be drained of inhabitants, to support the British arms in either Asia, Africa, or Europe.

Besides, what have we to do with setting the world at defiance? Our plan is commerce, and that, well attended to, will secure us the peace and friendship of all Europe; because it is the interest of all Europe to have America a free port. Her trade will always be a protection, and her barrenness of gold and silver secure her from invaders.

I challenge the warmest advocate for reconciliation to show a single advantage that this continent can reap by being connected with Great Britain. I repeat the challenge; not a single advantage is derived. Our corn will fetch its price in any market in Europe, and our imported goods must be paid for buy them where we will.

But the injuries and disadvantages which we sustain by that connection, are without number; and our duty to mankind at large, as well as to ourselves, instruct us to renounce the alliance: because, any submission to, or dependance on, Great Britain, tends directly to involve this Continent in European wars and quarrels, and set us at variance with nations who would otherwise seek our friendship, and against whom we have neither anger nor complaint. As Europe is our market for trade, we ought to form no partial connection with any part of it. It is the true interest of America to steer clear of European contentions, which she never can do, while, by her dependance on Britain, she is made the makeweight in the scale of British politics.

Europe is too thickly planted with Kingdoms to be long at peace, and whenever a war breaks out between England and any foreign power, the trade of America goes to ruin, *because of her connection with Britain.* The next war may not turn out like the last, and should it not, the advocates for reconciliation now will be wishing for separation then, because neutrality in that case would be a safer convoy than a man of war. Every thing that is right or reasonable pleads for separation. The blood of the slain, the weeping voice of nature cries, 'Tis Time to Part. Even the distance at which the Almighty hath placed England and America is a strong and natural proof that the authority of the one over the other, was never the design of Heaven. The time likewise at which the Continent was discovered, adds weight to the argument, and the manner in which it was peopled, encreases the force of it. The Reformation was preceded by the discovery of America: As if the Almighty graciously meant to open a sanctuary to the persecuted in future years, when home should afford neither friendship nor safety. . . .

'Tis repugnant to reason, to the universal order of things, to all examples from former ages, to suppose that this Continent can long remain subject to any external power. The most sanguine in Britain doth not think so. The utmost stretch of human wisdom cannot, at this time, compass a plan, short of separation, which can promise the continent even a year's security. Reconciliation is *now* a fallacious dream. Nature hath deserted the connection, and art cannot supply her place. For, as Milton wisely expresses, "never can true reconcilement grow where wounds of deadly hate have pierced so deep."

Every quiet method for peace hath been ineffectual. Our prayers have been rejected with disdain; and hath tended to convince us that nothing flatters vanity or confirms obstinacy in Kings more than repeated petitioning—and nothing hath contributed more than that very measure to make the Kings of Europe absolute. . . . Wherefore, since nothing but blows will do, for God's sake let us come to a final separation, and not leave the next generation to be cutting throats under the violated unmeaning names of parent and child. . . .

Small islands not capable of protecting themselves are the proper objects for government to take under their care; but there is something absurd, in supposing a Continent to be perpetually governed by an island. In no instance hath nature made the satellite larger than its primary planet; and as England and America, with respect to each other, reverse the common order of nature, it is evident that they belong to different systems. England to Europe: America to itself.

I am not induced by motives of pride, party, or resentment to espouse the doctrine of separation and independence; I am clearly, positively, and conscientiously persuaded that it is the true interest of this Continent to be so; that every thing short of *that* is mere patchwork, that it can afford no lasting felicity,—that it is leaving the sword to our children, and shrinking back at a time when a little more, a little further, would have rendered this Continent the glory of the earth. . . .

Ye that tell us of harmony and reconciliation, can ye restore to us the time that is past? Can ye give to prostitution its former innocence? neither can ye reconcile Britain and America. The last cord now is broken, the people of England are presenting addresses against us. There are injuries which nature cannot forgive; she would cease to be nature if she did. As well can the lover forgive the ravisher of his mistress, as the Continent forgive the murders of Britain. The Almighty hath implanted in us these unextinguishable feelings for good and wise purposes. They are the Guardians of his Image in our hearts. They distinguish us from the herd of common animals. The social compact would dissolve, and justice be extirpated from the earth, or have only a casual existence were we callous to the touches of affection. The robber and the murderer would often escape unpunished, did not the injuries which our tempers sustain, provoke us into justice.

O! ye that love mankind! Ye that dare oppose not only the tyranny but the tyrant, stand forth! Every spot of the old world is overrun with oppression. Freedom hath been hunted round the Globe. Asia and Africa have long expelled her. Europe regards her like a stranger, and England hath given her warning to depart. O! receive the fugitive, and prepare in time an asylum for mankind.

THE DECLARATION

OF INDEPENDENCE

. . . When a long train of abuses and usurpations, pursuing invariably the same Object evinces a design to reduce them under absolute Despotism, it is their right, it is their duty, to throw off such Government, and to provide new Guards for their future security.—1776.

*W*HEN IN THE COURSE of human events, it becomes necessary for one people to dissolve the political bands which have connected them with another, and to assume among the Powers of the earth, the separate and equal station to which the Laws of Nature and of Nature's God entitle them, a decent respect to the opinions of mankind requires that they should declare the causes which impel them to the separation.

We hold these truths to be self-evident, that all men are created equal, that they are endowed by their Creator with certain unalienable Rights, that among these are Life, Liberty and the pursuit of Happiness. That to secure these rights, Governments are instituted among Men deriving their just powers from the consent of the governed, That whenever any Form of Government becomes destructive of these ends, it is the Right of the People to alter or to abolish it, and to institute new Government, laying its foundation on such principles and organizing its powers in such form, as to them shall seem most likely to effect their Safety and Happiness. Prudence, indeed, will dictate that Governments long established should not be changed for light and transient causes; and accordingly all experience hath shewn, that mankind are more disposed to suffer, while evils are sufferable, than to right themselves by abolishing the forms to which they are accustomed. But when a long train of abuses and usurpations, pursuing invariably the same Object evinces a design to reduce them under absolute Despotism, it is their right, it is their duty, to throw off such Government, and to provide new Guards for their future security. Such has been the patient sufferance of these Colonies; and such is now the necessity which constrains them to alter their former Systems of Government. The history of the present King of Great Britain is a history of repeated injuries and usurpations, all having in direct object the establishment of an absolute Tyranny over these States. To prove this, let Facts be submitted to a candid world.

He has refused his Assent to Laws, the most wholesome and necessary for the public good.

He has forbidden his Governors to pass Laws of immediate and pressing importance, unless suspended in their operation till his Assent should be obtained; and when so suspended, he has utterly neglected to attend to them.

He has refused to pass other Laws for the accommodation of large districts of people, unless those people would relinquish the right of Representation in the Legislature, a right inestimable to them and formidable to tyrants only.

He has called together legislative bodies at places unusual, uncomfortable, and distant from the depository of their Public Records, for the sole purpose of fatiguing them into compliance with his measures.

He has dissolved Representative Houses repeatedly, for opposing with manly firmness his invasions on the rights of the people.

He has refused for a long time, after such dissolutions, to cause others to be elected; whereby the Legislative Powers, incapable of Annihilation, have returned to the People at large for their exercise;

the State remaining in the mean time exposed to all the dangers of invasion from without, and convulsions within.

He has endeavoured to prevent the population of these States; for that purpose obstructing the Laws of Naturalization of Foreigners; refusing to pass others to encourage their migration hither, and raising the conditions of new Appropriations of Lands.

He has obstructed the Administration of Justice, by refusing his Assent to Laws for establishing Judiciary Powers.

He has made Judges dependent on his Will alone, for the tenure of their offices, and the amount and payment of their salaries.

He has erected a multitude of New Offices, and sent hither swarms of Officers to harass our People, and eat out their substance.

He has kept among us, in times of peace, Standing Armies without the Consent of our legislature.

He has affected to render the Military independent of and superior to the Civil Power.

He has combined with others to subject us to a jurisdiction foreign to our constitution, and unacknowledged by our laws; giving his Assent to their Acts of pretended Legislation:

For quartering large bodies of armed troops among us:

For protecting them, by a mock Trial, from Punishment for any Murders which they should commit on the Inhabitants of these States:

For cutting off our Trade with all parts of the world:

For imposing Taxes on us without our Consent:

For depriving us in many cases, of the benefits of Trial by Jury:

For transporting us beyond Seas to be tried for pretended offences:

For abolishing the free System of English Laws in a neighbouring Province, establishing therein an Arbitrary government, and enlarging its Boundaries so as to render it at once an example and fit instrument for introducing the same absolute rule into these Colonies:

For taking away our Charters, abolishing our most valuable Laws and altering fundamentally the Forms of our Governments:

For suspending our own Legislatures, and declaring themselves invested with Power to legislate for us in all cases whatsoever.

He has abdicated Government here, by declaring us out of his Protection and waging War against us.

He has plundered our seas, ravaged our Coasts, burnt our towns, and destroyed the Lives of our people.

He is at this time transporting large Armies of foreign Mercenaries to compleat the works of death, desolation and tyranny, already begun with circumstances of Cruelty & perfidy scarcely paralleled in the most barbarous ages, and totally unworthy the Head of a civilized nation.

He has constrained our fellow Citizens taken Captive on the high Seas to bear Arms against their Country, to become the executioners of their friends and Brethren, or to fall themselves by their Hands.

He has excited domestic insurrections amongst us, and has endeavoured to bring on the inhabitants of our frontiers, the merciless Indian Savages, whose known rule of warfare, is an undistinguished destruction of all ages, sexes and conditions.

In every stage of these Oppressions We have Petitioned for Redress in the most humble terms: Our repeated Petitions have been answered only by repeated injury. A Prince, whose character is thus marked by every act which may define a Tyrant, is unfit to be the ruler of a free People.

Nor have We been wanting in attentions to our British brethren. We have warned them from time to time of attempts by their legislature to extend an unwarrantable jurisdiction over us. We have reminded them of the circumstances of our emigration and settlement here. We have appealed to their native justice and magnanimity, and we have conjured them by the ties of our common kindred to disavow these usurpations, which would inevitably interrupt our connections and correspondence. They too have been deaf to the voice of justice and of consanguinity. We must, therefore, acquiesce in the necessity, which denounces our Separation, and hold them, as we hold the rest of mankind, Enemies in War, in Peace Friends.

We, therefore, the Representatives of the United States of America, in General Congress, Assembled, appealing to the Supreme Judge of the world for the rectitude of our intentions, do, in the Name, and by Authority of the good People of these Colonies, solemnly publish and declare, That these United Colonies are, and of Right ought to be Free and Independent States; that they are Absolved from all Allegiance to the British Crown, and that all political connection between them and the State of Great Britain, is and ought to be totally dissolved; and that as Free and Independent States, they have full Power to levy War, conclude Peace, contract Alliances, establish Commerce, and to do all other Acts and Things which Independent States may of right do.

And for the support of this Declaration, with a firm reliance on the protection of divine Providence, we mutually pledge to each other our Lives, our Fortunes and our sacred Honor.

II.   Neutralist State

The Declaration of Independence did not solve the essential issue between Dickinson and Paine, for the newly independent United States contracted an alliance with France, England's old enemy, and its success owed much to French help. Afterward, a number of Americans still had doubts as to whether their country could have a life outside the European political system.

But in 1789, revolution swept France. Government succeeded government, each more radical than the last. In 1793, when the deposed king, Louis XVI, was beheaded, England and a coalition of continental monarchies went to war with her, and Americans faced the question of whether or not to carry out the treaty of alliance and rally to France's side. Since some Americans sympathized with the French revolutionaries while others were scandalized by them, as were European conservatives, their debates touched as much on national ideals as on more practical matters.

Within George Washington's cabinet, Secretary of the Treasury Alexander Hamilton was anti-French, Secretary of State Thomas Jefferson pro-French. In presenting their contrasting opinions to the President, they rang every change, appealing to law, morality, national interest, national prestige, and public opinion. Like Dickinson and Paine, however, they argued from essentially similar premises.

Washington settled the issue by proclaiming neutrality and, in effect, treating the alliance as dead. In his Farewell Address, which Hamilton helped compose, he explained his policy and why he thought it should be continued. His speech became the fundamental statement of American neutralism.

ALEXANDER HAMILTON AND

THOMAS JEFFERSON ON

ALLIANCE WITH

REVOLUTIONARY FRANCE

It does not appear necessary to precipitate the fixing of our relations to France beyond the possibility of retraction.
                    —ALEXANDER HAMILTON, 1793.

T HE TREATIES BETWEEN the United States and France were made with His Most Christian Majesty, his heirs and successors. The government of France, which existed at the time those treaties were made, gave way, in the first instance, to a new constitution, formed by the representatives of the nation, and accepted by the king, which went into regular operation. Of a sudden, a tumultuous rising took place. The king was seized, imprisoned, and declared to be suspended by the authority of the National Assembly; a body delegated to exercise the legislative functions of the already established government—in no shape authorized to divest any other of the constituted authorities of its legal capacities or powers. So far, then, what was done was a manifest assumption of power.

Letter to President Washington from Alexander Hamilton, Secretary of the Treasury, April, 1793. John C. Hamilton, Ed., *The Works of Alexander Hamilton*. New York, 1851, vol. IV, pp. 363-379.

To justify it, it is alleged to have been necessary for the safety of the nation, to prevent the success of a counter-revolution mediated or patronized by the king.

On the other side, it is affirmed that the whole transaction was merely the execution of a plan which had been for some time projected, and had been gradually ripening, to bring about an abolition of the royalty and the establishment of a republican government.

No satisfactory proof is known to have been produced to fix upon the king the charges which have been brought against him. . . . In the last place, . . . [he] has been tried and condemned by the convention, and has suffered death.

Whether he has suffered justly or unjustly, whether he has been a guilty tyrant or an unfortunate victim, is at least a problem. There certainly can be no hazard in affirming, that no proof has yet come to light sufficient to establish a belief that the death of Louis is an act of national justice.

It appears to be regarded in a different light throughout Europe, and by a numerous and respectable part, if not by a majority, of the people of the United States.

Almost all Europe is or seems likely to be armed in opposition to the present rulers of France, with the declared or implied intention of restoring, if possible, the royalty in the successor of the deceased monarch.

The present war, then, turns essentially on the point—What shall be the future government of France? Shall the royal authority be restored in the person of the successor of Louis, or shall a republic be constituted in exclusion of it?

Thus stand the material facts which regard the origin of our connections with France, and the obligations or dispensations that now exist.

They have been stated, not with a view to indicate a definitive opinion concerning the propriety of the conduct of the present rulers of France, but to show that the course of the revolution there has been attended with circumstances, which militate against a full conviction of its having been brought to its present stage by such a *free, regular,* and *deliberate* act of the nation, and with such a spirit of justice and humanity, as ought to silence all scruples about the validity of what has been done, and the morality of aiding it, if consistent with policy.

This great and important question arises out of the facts which have been stated:

Are the United States bound, by the principles of the laws of nations, to consider the treaties heretofore made with France as in present force and operation between them and the actual governing powers of the French nation? or may they elect to consider their operation as suspended, reserving also a right to judge finally whether any such changes have happened in the political affairs of France, as may justify a renunciation of those treaties?

It is believed that they have an option to consider the operation of those treaties as suspended, and will have eventually a right to renounce them, if such changes shall take place as can *bona fide* be pronounced *to render* a continuance of the connections which result from them disadvantageous or dangerous. . . .

Nothing can be more evident than that the existing forms of government of two nations may enter far into the motives of a real treaty. Two republics may contract an alliance, the principal inducement to which may be a similarity of constitutions, producing a common interest to defend their mutual rights and liberties. A change of the government of one of them into a monarchy or despotism may destroy the inducement and the main link of common interest. Two monarchies may form an alliance on a like principle, their common defence against a powerful neighboring republic. The change of the government of one of the allies may destroy the source of common sympathy and common interest, and render it prudent for the other ally to renounce the connection and seek to fortify itself in some other quarter.

Two nations may form an alliance because each has confidence in the energy and efficacy of the government of the other. A revolution may subject one of them to a different form of government—feeble, fluctuating, and turbulent, liable to provoke wars, and very little fitted to repel them. Even the connections of a nation with other foreign powers may enter into the motives of an alliance with it. If a dissolution of ancient connections shall have been a consequence of a revolution of government, the external political relations of the parties may have become so varied as to occasion an incompatibility of the alliance with the power, which had changed its constitution with the other connections of its ally—connections perhaps essential to its welfare.

In such cases, reason, which is the touchstone of all similar maxims, would dictate that the party whose government had remained stationary, would have a right under a *bona fide* conviction that the change in the situation of the other party would render a future connection detrimental or dangerous, to declare the connection dissolved. . . .

If the opinions of writers be consulted, they will, as far as they go, confirm the sense of the maxim which is here contended for. . . . Vatel, who is the most systematic of the writers on the laws of nations, lays down the qualification in the greatest latitude. . . . "*The ally remains the ally of the state*, notwithstanding the change which has happened in it. However, when this change renders the alliance *useless, dangerous*, or *disagreeable*, it may renounce it; for it may say, upon a good foundation, that it would not have entered into an alliance with that nation had it been under the present form of government." . . .

The conclusion from the whole is, that there is an option in the United States to hold the operation of the treaties suspended; and that in the event, if the form of government established in France shall be such as to render a continuance of the treaties contrary to the interest of the United States, they may be renounced.

If there be such an option, there are strong reasons to show that the character and interests of the United States require, that they should pursue the course of holding the operation of the treaties suspended.

Their character:

Because it was from Louis XVI, the then sovereign of the country, that they received those succors which were so important in the establishment of their independence and liberty. It was with him, his heirs, and successors, that they contracted their engagements—by which they obtained those precious succors.

It is enough, on their part, to respect the right of the nation to change its government, so far as not to side with the successors of the dethroned prince; as to receive their ambassador, and keep up an amicable intercourse; as to be willing to render every good office, not contrary to the duties of a real neutrality.

To throw their weight into the scale of the new government, would, it is to be feared, be considered by mankind as not consistent with a decent regard to the relations which subsisted between them and Louis XVI; as not consistent with a due sense of the services they received from that unfortunate prince; as not consistent with national delicacy and decorum.

The character of the United States may also be concerned in keeping clear of any connection with the present government of France, in other views.

A struggle for liberty is in itself respectable and glorious; when conducted with magnanimity, justice, and humanity, it ought to command the admiration of every friend to human nature; but if sullied by crimes and extravagancies, it loses its respectability. Though success may rescue it from infamy, it cannot, in the opinion of the sober part of mankind, attach to it much positive merit or praise. But in the event of a want of success, a general execration must attend it.

It appears, thus far, but too probable, that the pending revolution of France has sustained some serious blemishes. There is too much ground to anticipate, that a sentence uncommonly severe will be passed upon it if it fails.

Will it be well for the United States to expose their reputation to the *issue*, by implicating themselves as associates? Will their reputation be promoted by a successful issue? What will it suffer by the reverse?

These questions suggest very serious considerations to a mind anxious for the reputation of the country—anxious that it may emulate a character of sobriety, moderation, justice, and love of order.

The *interest* of the United States seems to dictate the course recommended, in many ways:

I. In reference to their character, from the considerations already stated.

II. In reference to their peace. . . .

How far the parties opposed to France may think fit to treat us as enemies . . . is a problem which experience only can solve; the solution of which will probably be regulated by their views of their own interest—by the circumstances which may occur; and it is far from impossible that these will restrain them, so long as we, in fact, take no active part in favor of France.

But if there be an option to avoid it, it can hardly be wise to incur so great an additional risk and embarrassment, to implicate ourselves in the perplexities which may follow. . . .

When all Europe is, or is likely to be, armed in opposition to the authority of the present government of France, would it not be to carry theory to an extreme, to pronounce that the United States are *under* an *absolute* indispensable obligation, not only to acknowledge respectfully the authority of that government, but to admit the immediate operation of treaties, which would constitute them at once its ally?

Prudence, at least, seems to dictate the course of *reserving* the question, in order that further reflection and a more complete development of circumstances shall enable us to make a decision both *right* and *safe*. It does not appear necessary to precipitate the fixing of our relations to France beyond the possibility of retraction. It is putting too suddenly too much to hazard.

*... The treaties are still binding, notwithstanding the change of gov-
ernment in France. . . .*   —THOMAS JEFFERSON, 1793.

I PROCEED, in compliance with the requisition of the President, to
give an opinion in writing on the general Question, Whether the U.S.
have a right to renounce their treaties with France, or to hold them
suspended till the government of that country shall be established?

In the Consultation at the President's on the 19th inst. the Secretary of the Treasury took the following positions & consequences.
"France was a monarchy when we entered into treaties with it: but it
has now declared itself a Republic, & is preparing a Republican form
of government. As it may issue in a Republic, or a Military despotism,
or in something else which may possibly render our alliance with it
dangerous to ourselves, we have a right of election to renounce the
treaty altogether, or to declare it suspended till their government
shall be settled in the form it is ultimately to take; and then we may
judge whether we will call the treaties into operation again, or declare them forever null. . . ."

If I do not subscribe to the soundness of this reasoning, I do most
fully to its ingenuity.—I shall now lay down the principles which
according to my understanding govern the case.

I consider the people who constitute a society or nation as the
source of all authority in that nation, as free to transact their common
concerns by any agents they think proper, to change these agents indi-
vidually, or the organisation of them in form or function whenever
they please: that all the acts done by those agents under the authority
of the nation, are the acts of the nation, are obligatory on them, & en-

Letter to President Washington from Thomas Jefferson, Secretary of State, April, 1793.
Paul Leicester Ford, ed., *The Works of Thomas Jefferson*. New York, 1904, vol. VII,
pp. 283-300.

sure to their use, & can in no wise be annulled or affected by any
change in the form of the government, or of the persons administer-
ing it. Consequently the Treaties between the U.S. and France, were
not treaties between the U.S. & Louis Capet, but between the two
nations of America & France, and the nations remaining in existance,
tho' both of them have since changed their forms of government, the
treaties are not annulled by these changes.

The Law of nations, by which this question is to be determined, is
composed of three branches. 1. The Moral Law of our nature. 2. The
Usages of nations. 3. Their special Conventions. The first of these
only, concerns this question, that is to say the Moral law to which
Man has been subjected by his creator, & of which his feelings, or
Conscience as it is sometimes called, are the evidence with which his
creator has furnished him. The Moral duties which exist between
individual and individual in a state of nature, accompany them into a
state of society & the aggregate of the duties of all the individuals
composing the society constitutes the duties of that society towards
any other; so that between society & society the same moral duties
exist as did between the individuals composing them while in an un-
associated state, their maker not having released them from those
duties on their forming themselves into a nation. Compacts then between nation & nation are obligatory on them by the same moral law
which obliges individuals to observe their compacts. There are circumstances however which sometimes excuse the non-performance of
contracts between man & man: so are there also between nation &
nation. When performance, for instance, becomes *impossible*, non-
performance is not immoral. So if performance becomes *self-destruc-
tive* to the party, the law of self-preservation overrules the laws of
obligation to others. For the reality of these principles I appeal to the
true fountains of evidence, the head & heart of every rational & honest
man. It is there Nature has written her moral laws, & where every
man may read them for himself. He will never read there the permis-
sion to annul his obligations for a time, or for ever, whenever they

become "dangerous, useless, or disagreeable." Certainly not when merely *useless* or *disagreeable*, as seems to be said in . . . Vattel. . . ., and tho he may under certain degrees of *danger*, yet the danger must be imminent, & the degree great. Of these, it is true, that nations are to be judges for themselves, since no one nation has a right to sit in judgment over another. But the tribunal of our consciences remains, & that also of the opinion of the world. These will revise the sentence we pass in our own case, & as we respect these, we must see that in judging ourselves we have honestly done the part of impartial & vigorous judges.

But Reason, which gives this right of self-liberation from a contract in certain cases, has subjected it to certain just limitations.

I. The danger which absolves us must be great, inevitable & imminent. Is such the character of that now apprehended from our treaties with France? What is that danger? 1. Is it that if their government issues in a military despotism, an alliance with them may taint us with despotic principles? But their government, when we allied ourselves to it, was a perfect despotism, civil & military, yet the treaties were made in that very state of things, & therefore that danger can furnish no just cause. 2. Is it that their government may issue in a republic, and too much strengthen our republican principles? But this is the hope of the great mass of our constituents, & not their dread. They do not look with longing to the happy mean of a limited monarchy. 3. But says the doctrine I am combating, the change the French are undergoing may possibly end in something we know not what, and bring on us danger we know not whence. In short it may end in a Rawhead & bloody-bones in the dark. Very well. Let Rawhead & bloody-bones come, & then we shall be justified in making our peace with him, by renouncing our antient friends & his enemies. For observe, it is not the *possibility of danger*, which absolves a party from his contract: for that possibility always exists, & in every case. It existed in the present one at the moment of making the contract. If *possibilities* would avoid contracts, there never could be a valid contract. For possibilities hang over everything. Obligation is not suspended, till the danger is become real, & the moment of it so imminent, that we can no longer avoid decision without forever losing the opportunity to do it. But can a danger which has not yet taken its shape, which does not yet exist, & never may exist, which cannot therefore be defined, can such a danger I ask, be so imminent that if we fail to pronounce on it in this moment we can never have another opportunity of doing it?

4. The danger apprehended, is it that, the treaties remaining valid, the clause guarantying their West India islands will engage us in the war? But Does the Guarantee engage us to enter into the war in any event?

Are we to enter into it before we are called on by our allies? Have we been called on by them?—shall we ever be called on? Is it their interest to call on us?

Can they call on us before their islands are invaded, or imminently threatened?

If they can save them themselves, have they a right to call on us?

Are we obliged to go to war at once, without trying peaceable negociations with their enemy?

If all these questions be against us, there are still others behind.

Are we in a condition to go to war?

Can we be expected to begin before we are in condition?

Will the islands be lost if we do not save them? Have we the means of saving them?

If we cannot save them are we bound to go to war for a desperate object ... ?

Many, if not most of these questions offer grounds of doubt whether the clause of guarantee will draw us into the war. Consequently if this be the danger apprehended, it is not yet certain enough to authorize us in sound morality to declare, at this moment, the treaties null. ...

II. A second limitation on our right of releasing ourselves is that we are to do it from so much of the treaties only as is bringing great & inevitable danger on us, & not from the residue, allowing to the other party a right at the same time to determine whether on our non-compliance with that part they will declare the whole void. This right they would have, but we should not. . . .

If in withholding a compliance with any part of the treaties, we do it without just cause or compensation, we give to France a cause of war, and so become associated in it on the other side. An injured friend is the bitterest of foes, & France had not discovered either timidity, or over-much forbearance on the late occasions. Is this the position we wish to take for our constituents? It is certainly not the one they would take for themselves. . . .

The Republic of the U. S. allied itself with France when under a despotic government. She changes her government, declares it shall be a Republic, prepares a form of Republic extremely free, and in the mean time is governing herself as such, and it is proposed that America shall declare the treaties void because "it may say with truth that it would not have allied itself with that nation, if it had been under the present form of it's government!" Who is the American who can say with truth that he would not have allied himself to France if she had been a republic? or that a Republic of any form would be as *disagreeable* as her antient despotism?

Upon the whole I conclude

That the treaties are still binding, nothwithstanding the change of government in France: that no part of them, but the clause of guarantee, holds up *danger*, even at a distance.

And consequently that a liberation from no other part could be proposed in any case: that if that clause may ever bring *danger*, it is neither extreme, nor imminent, nor even probable: that the authority for renouncing a treaty, when *useless* or *disagreeable*, is either misunderstood, or in opposition to itself, to all their writers, & to every moral feeling: that were it not so, these treaties are in fact neither useless nor disagreeable. . . .

WASHINGTON'S FAREWELL ADDRESS

It is our true policy to steer clear of permanent alliances with any portion of the foreign world, so far, I mean, as we are now at liberty to do it; for let me not be understood as capable of patronizing infidelity to existing engagements. GEORGE WASHINGTON, 1796.

IN LOOKING FORWARD to the moment which is intended to terminate the career of my political life my feelings do not permit me to suspend the deep acknowledgment of that debt of gratitude which I owe to my beloved country for the many honors it has conferred upon me; still more for the steadfast confidence with which it has supported me, and for the opportunities I have thence enjoyed of manifesting my inviolable attachment by services faithful and persevering, though in usefulness unequal to my zeal. If benefits have resulted to our country from these services, let it always be remembered to your praise and as an instructive example in our annals that under circumstances in which the passions, agitated in every direction, were liable to mislead; amidst appearances sometimes dubious; vicissitudes of fortune often discouraging; in situations in which not unfrequently want of success has countenanced the spirit of criticism, the constancy of your support was the essential prop of the efforts and a guaranty of the plans by which they were effected. Profoundly penetrated with this idea, I shall carry it with me to my grave as a strong incitement to unceasing vows that Heaven may con-

September 17, 1796. James D. Richardson, ed., *Messages and Papers of the Presidents.* Washington, D.C., 1897, vol. I, pp. 214-224.

tinue to you the choicest tokens of its beneficence; that your union and brotherly affection may be perpetual; that the free Constitution which is the work of your hands may be sacredly maintained; that its administration in every department may be stamped with wisdom and virtue; that, in fine, the happiness of the people of these States, under the auspices of liberty, may be made complete by so careful a preservation and so prudent a use of this blessing as will acquire to them the glory of recommending it to the applause, the affection, and adoption of every nation which is yet a stranger to it.

Here, perhaps, I ought to stop. But a solicitude for your welfare which can not end but with my life, and the apprehension of danger natural to that solicitude, urge me on an occasion like the present to offer your solemn contemplation and to recommend to your frequent review some sentiments which are the result of much reflection, of no inconsiderable observation, and which appear to me all important to the permanency of your felicity as a people. These will be offered to you with the more freedom as you can only see in them the disinterested warnings of a parting friend, who can possibly have no personal motive to bias his counsel. . . .

Interwoven as is the love of liberty with every ligament of your hearts, no recommendation of mine is necessary to fortify or confirm the attachment.

The unity of government which constitutes you one people is also now dear to you. It is justly so, for it is a main pillar in the edifice of your real independence, the support of your tranquility at home, your peace abroad, of your safety, of your prosperity, of that very liberty which you so highly prize. But as it is easy to foresee that from different causes and from different quarters much pains will be taken, many artifices employed, to weaken in your minds the conviction of this truth, as this is the point in your political fortress against which the batteries of internal and external enemies will be most constantly and actively (though often covertly and insidiously) directed, it is of infinite moment that you should properly estimate the immense value of your national union to your collective and individual happiness; that you should cherish a cordial, habitual, and immovable attachment to it; accustoming yourselves to think and speak of it as of the palladium of your political safety and prosperity; watching for its preservation with jealous anxiety; discountenancing whatever may suggest even a suspicion that it can in any event be abandoned, and indignantly frowning upon the first dawning of every attempt to alienate any portion of our country from the rest or to enfeeble the sacred ties which now link together the various parts.

For this you have every inducement of sympathy and interest. Citizens by birth or choice of a common country, that country has a right to concentrate your affections. The name of American, which belongs to you in your national capacity, must always exalt the just pride of patriotism more than any appellation derived from local discriminations. With slight shades of difference, you have the same religion, manners, habits, and political principles. You have in a common cause fought and triumphed together. The independence and liberty you possess are the work of joint councils and joint efforts, of common dangers, sufferings, and successes. . . .

In contemplating the causes which may disturb our union it occurs as matter of serious concern that any ground should have been furnished for characterizing parties by *geographical* discriminations—*Northern* and *Southern, Atlantic* and *Western*—whence designing men may endeavor to excite a belief that there is a real difference of local interests and views. . . .

To the efficacy and permanency of your union a government for the whole is indispensable. . . . Respect for its authority, compliance with its laws, acquiescence in its measures, are duties enjoined by the fundamental maxims of true liberty. The basis of our political systems is the right of the people to make and to alter their constitutions of government. But the constitution which at any time exists till changed by an explicit and authentic act of the whole people is sacredly obligatory upon all. The very idea of the power and the right of the people to establish government presupposes the duty of every individual to obey the established government.

All obstructions to the execution of the laws, all combinations and associations, under whatever plausible character with the real design to direct, control, counteract, or awe the regular deliberation and action of the constituted authorities, are destructive of this fundamental principle and of fatal tendency. They serve to organize faction; to give it an artificial and extraordinary force; to put in the place of the delegated will of the nation the will of a party, often a small but artful and enterprising minority of the community, and, according to the alternate triumphs of different parties, to make the public administration the mirror of the ill-concerted and incongruous projects of faction rather than the organ of consistent and wholesome plans, digested by common counsels and modified by mutual interests.

However combinations or associations of the above description may now and then answer popular ends, they are likely in the course of time and things to become potent engines by which cunning, ambitious, and unprincipled men will be enabled to subvert the power of the people, and to usurp for themselves the reins of government, destroying afterwards the very engines which have lifted them to unjust dominion.

Toward the preservation of your Government and the permanency of your present happy state, it is requisite not only that you steadily discountenance irregular oppositions to its acknowledged authority, but also that you resist with care the spirit of innovation upon its principles, however specious the pretexts. One method of assault may be to effect in the forms of the Constitution alterations which will impair the energy of the system, and thus to undermine what can not be directly overthrown. In all the changes to which you may be invited remember that time and habit are at least as necessary to fix the true character of governments as of other human institutions; that experience is the surest standard by which to test the real tendency of the existing constitution of a country; that facility in changes upon the credit of mere hypothesis and opinion exposes to perpetual change, from the endless variety of hypothesis and opinion; and remember especially that for the efficient management of your common interests in a country so extensive as ours a government of as much vigor as is consistent with the perfect security of liberty is indispensable. Liberty itself will find in such a government, with powers properly distributed and adjusted, its surest guardian. It is, indeed, little else than a name where the government is too feeble to withstand the enterprises of faction, to confine each member of the society within the limits prescribed by the laws, and to maintain all in the secure and tranquil enjoyment of the rights of person and property.

I have already intimated to you the danger of parties in the State, with particular reference to the founding of them on geographical discriminations. Let me now take a more comprehensive view, and warn you in the most solemn manner against the baneful effects of the spirit of party generally. . . .

It serves always to distract the public councils and enfeeble the public administration. It agitates the community with ill-founded jealousies and false alarms; kindles the animosity of one part against another; foments occasionally riot and insurrection. It opens the door to foreign influence and corruption, which find a facilitated access to the government itself through the channels of party passion. Thus the policy and the will of one country are subjected to the policy and will of another. . . .

It is important, likewise, that the habits of thinking in a free country should inspire caution in those intrusted with its administration to confine themselves within their respective constitutional spheres, avoiding in the exercise of the powers of one department to encroach upon another. The spirit of encroachment tends to consolidate the powers of all the departments in one, and thus to create, whatever the form of government, a real despotism. . . .

Of all the dispositions and habits which lead to political prosperity, religion and morality are indispensable supports. In vain would that man claim the tribute of patriotism who should labor to subvert these great pillars of human happiness—these firmest props of the duties of men and citizens. The mere politician, equally with the pious man, ought to respect and to cherish them. A volume could not trace all their connections with private and public felicity. Let it simply be asked, Where is the security for property, for reputation, for life, if the sense of religious obligation *desert* the oaths which are the instruments of investigation in courts of justice? And let us with caution indulge the supposition that morality can be maintained without religion. Whatever may be conceded to the influence of refined education on minds of peculiar structure, reason and experience both forbid us to expect that national morality can prevail in exclusion of religious principle.

It is substantially true that virtue or morality is a necessary spring of popular government. The rule indeed extends with more or less force to every species of free government. Who that is a sincere friend to it can look with indifference upon attempts to shake the foundation of the fabric? Promote, then, as an object of primary importance, institutions for the general diffusion of knowledge. In proportion as the structure of a government gives force to public opinion, it is essential that public opinion should be enlightened.

As a very important source of strength and security, cherish public credit. One method of preserving it is to use it as sparingly as possible, avoiding occasions of expense by cultivating peace, but remembering also that timely disbursements to prepare for danger frequently prevent much greater disbursements to repel it; avoiding likewise the accumulation of debt, not only by shunning occasions of expense, but by vigorous exertions in time of peace to discharge the debts which unavoidable wars have occasioned, not ungenerously throwing upon posterity the burthen which we ourselves ought to bear. . . .

Observe good faith and justice toward all nations. Cultivate peace and harmony with all. Religion and morality enjoin this conduct. And can it be that good policy does not equally enjoin it? It will be worthy of a free, enlightened, and at no distant period a great nation to give to mankind the magnanimous and too novel example of a people always guided by an exalted justice and benevolence. Who can doubt that in the course of time and things the fruits of such a plan would richly repay any temporary advantages which might be lost by a steady adherence to it? Can it be that Providence has not connected the permanent felicity of a nation with its virtue? The experiment, at least, is recommended by every sentiment which ennobles human nature. Alas! is it rendered impossible by its vices?

In the execution of such a plan nothing is more essential than that permanent, inveterate antipathies against particular nations and passionate attachments for others should be excluded, and that in place of them just and amicable feelings toward all should be cultivated. The nation which indulges toward another an habitual hatred or an habitual fondness is in some degree a slave. It is a slave to its animosity or to its affection, either of which is sufficient to lead it astray from its duty and its interest. Antipathy in one nation against another disposes each more readily to offer insult and injury, to lay hold of slight causes of umbrage, and to be haughty and intractable when accidental or trifling occasions of dispute occur.

Hence frequent collisions, obstinate, envenomed, and bloody contests. The nation prompted by ill will and resentment sometimes impels to war the government contrary to the best calculations of policy. The government sometimes participates in the national propensity, and adopts through passion what reason would reject. At other times it makes the animosity of the nation subservient to projects of hostility, instigated by pride, ambition, and other sinister and pernicious motives. The peace often, sometimes perhaps the liberty, of nations has been the victim.

So, likewise, a passionate attachment of one nation for another produces a variety of evils. Sympathy for the favorite nation, facilitating the illusion of an imaginary common interest in cases where no real common interest exists, and infusing into one the enmities of the other, betrays the former into a participation in the quarrels and wars of the latter without adequate inducement or justification. It leads also to concessions to the favorite nation of privileges denied to others, which is apt doubly to injure the nation making the concessions by unnecessarily parting with what ought to have been retained, and by exciting jealousy, ill will, and a disposition to retaliate in the parties from whom equal privileges are withheld; and it gives to ambitious, corrupted, or deluded citizens (who devote themselves to the favorite nation) facility to betray or sacrifice the interests of their own country without odium, sometimes even with popularity, gilding with the appearances of a virtuous sense of obligation, a commendable deference for public opinion, or a laudable zeal for public good the base or foolish compliances of ambition, corruption, or infatuation.

As avenues to foreign influence in innumerable ways, such attachments are particularly alarming to the truly enlightened and independent patriot. How many opportunities do they afford to tamper with domestic factions, to practice the arts of seduction, to mislead public opinion, to influence or awe the public councils! Such an attachment of a small or weak toward a great and powerful nation dooms the former to be the satellite of the latter. Against the insidious wiles of foreign influence (I conjure you to believe me, fellow-citizens) the jealousy of a free people ought to be *constantly* awake, since history and experience prove that foreign influence is one of the most baneful foes of republican government. But that jealousy, to be useful, must be impartial, else it becomes the instrument of the very influence to be avoided, instead of a defense against it. Excessive partiality for one foreign nation and excessive dislike of another cause those whom they actuate to see danger only on one side, and serve to veil and even second the arts of influence on the other. Real patriots who may resist the intrigues of the favorite are liable to become suspected and odious, while its tools and dupes usurp the applause and confidence of the people to surrender their interests.

The great rule of conduct for us in regard to foreign nations is, in extending our commercial relations to have with them as little *political* connection as possible. So far as we have already formed engagements let them be fulfilled with perfect good faith. Here let us stop.

Europe has a set of primary interests which to us have none or a very remote relation. Hence she must be engaged in frequent controversies, the causes of which are essentially foreign to our concerns. Hence, therefore, it must be unwise in us to implicate ourselves by artificial ties in the ordinary vicissitudes of her politics or the ordinary combinations and collisions of her friendships or enmities.

Our detached and distant situation invites and enables us to pursue a different course. If we remain one people, under an efficient government, the period is not far off when we may defy material injury from external annoyance; when we may take such an attitude as will cause the neutrality we may at any time resolve upon to be scrupulously respected; when belligerent nations, under the impossibility of making acquisitions upon us, will not lightly hazard the giving us provocation; when we may choose peace or war, as our interest, guided by justice, shall counsel.

Why forego the advantages of so peculiar a situation? Why quit our own to stand upon foreign ground? Why, by interweaving our destiny with that of any part of Europe, entangle our peace and prosperity in the toils of European ambition, rivalship, interest, humor, or caprice?

It is our true policy to steer clear of permanent alliances with any portion of the foreign world, so far, I mean, as we are now at liberty to do it; for let me not be understood as capable of patronizing infidelity to existing engagements. I hold the maxim no less applicable to public than to private affairs that honesty is always the best policy. I repeat, therefore, let those engagements be observed in their genuine sense. But in my opinion it is unnecessary and would be unwise to extend them.

Taking care always to keep ourselves by suitable establishments on a respectable defensive posture, we may safely trust to temporary alliances for extraordinary emergencies.

Harmony, liberal intercourse with all nations are recommended by policy, humanity, and interest. But even our commercial policy should hold an equal and impartial hand, neither seeking nor granting exclusive favors or preferences; consulting the natural course of things; diffusing and diversifying by gentle means the streams of commerce, but forcing nothing; establishing with powers so disposed, in order to give trade a stable course, to define the rights of our merchants, and to enable the Government to support them, conventional rules of intercourse, the best that present circumstances and mutual opinion will permit, but temporary and liable to be from time to time abandoned or varied as experience and circumstances shall dictate; constantly keeping in view that it is folly in one nation to look for disinterested favors from another; that it must pay with a portion of its independence for whatever it may accept under that character; that by such acceptance it may place itself in the condition of having given equivalents for nominal favors, and yet of being reproached with ingratitude for not giving more. There can be no greater error than to expect or calculate upon real favors from nation to nation. It is an illusion which experience must cure, which a just pride ought to discard.

In offering to you, my countrymen, these counsels of an old and affectionate friend I dare not hope they will make the strong and lasting impression I could wish—that they will control the usual current of the passions or prevent our nation from running the course which has hitherto marked the destiny of nations. But if I may even flatter myself that they may be productive of some partial benefit, some occasional good—that they may now and then recur to moderate the fury of party spirit, to warn against the mischiefs of foreign intrigue, to guard against the impostures of pretended patriotism— this hope will be a full recompense for the solicitude for your welfare by which they have been dictated.

How far in the discharge of my official duties I have been guided by the principles which have been delineated the public records and other evidences of my conduct must witness to you and to the world. To myself, the assurance of my own conscience is that I have at least believed myself to be guided by them.

In relation to the still subsisting war in Europe my proclamation of the 22d of April, 1793, is the index to my plan. Sanctioned by your approving voice and by that of your representatives in both

Houses of Congress, the spirit of that measure has continually governed me, uninfluenced by any attempts to deter or divert me from it.

After deliberate examination, with the aid of the best lights I could
obtain, I was well satisfied that our country, under all the circumstances of the case, had a right to take, and was bound in duty and
interest to take, a neutral position. Having taken it, I determined as
far as should depend upon me to maintain it with moderation, perse-
verance, and firmness. . . .

The duty of holding a neutral conduct may be inferred, without
anything more, from the obligation which justice and humanity impose on every nation, in cases in which it is free to act, to maintain
inviolate the relations of peace and amity toward other nations.

The inducements of interest for observing that conduct will best
be referred to your own reflections and experience. With me a pre-
dominant motive has been to endeavor to gain time to our country
to settle and mature its yet recent institutions, and to progress without interruption to that degree of strength and consistency which is
necessary to give it, humanly speaking, the command of its own
fortunes.

III. Leader of a Neutral Bloc

In the aftermath of the wars touched off by the French Revolution, the Spanish empire in the Americas disintegrated. From Mexico to Chile, colony after colony declared independence, many borrowing the language of the American Declaration of 1776 and adopting constitutions modeled on that of the United States.

Although American sympathies were almost wholly on the side of the rebels, the government was circumspect. For a long time it seemed possible that Spain might put down these independence movements. Having strong moral backing from three powers of the Holy Alliance —Russia, Prussia, and Austria-Hungary—she appeared to have a good chance of getting material aid in her struggle, if the British, controlling the Atlantic, did not oppose it. Until it became clearer that the United States would not be backing a losing cause and risking a clash not only with Spain but with all Europe, President James Monroe and his Secretary of State, John Quincy Adams, preferred not to side with the rebels. In addition, since Spain was eager to prevent the United States from supporting the independence movements, they found it profitable to wait. The Spaniards made many concessions, especially in regard to boundaries in North America.

This policy provoked debate. Henry Clay, a senator from Kentucky, an ardent nationalist, and a presidential aspirant, became the spokesman for those who held that the United States had an imperial mission and destiny in the Western Hemisphere. Adams, a cold, brilliant New Englander, son of a president, himself soon to be president, replied to him, arguing not that the Administration's course was expedient but that it was morally right. America's mission, he declared, was not to rule an empire limited in territorial extent but to stand apart as a model, exercising its influence as an example upon the entire world. The Monroe Doctrine of 1823 provided a formula postponing a decision between these two views.

HENRY CLAY AND

JOHN QUINCY ADAMS ON

AMERICA'S MISSION

IN THE HEMISPHERE

. . . Let us no longer watch the nod of any European politician; let us become real and true Americans, and place ourselves at the head of the American system. —HENRY CLAY, 1820.

. . . . *M*R. CLAY AROSE and said: The proposition, to recognize the independent governments of South America, offers a subject of as great importance as any which could claim the deliberate consideration of this house.

Mr. Clay then went on to say, that it appeared to him the object of this government, heretofore, had been, so to manage its affairs, in regard to South America, as to produce an effect on its existing negotiations with the parent country. . . .

After the return of our commissioners from South America; after they had all agreed in attesting the fact of independent sovereignty being exercised by the government of Buenos Ayres; the whole nation looked forward to the recognition of the independence of that

Speech in the House of Representatives, May 10, 1820. *Annals of the Congress of the United States,* 16th Congress, 1st Session, pp. 2223-2230.

country, as the policy which the government ought to pursue. He appealed to every member to say, whether there was not a general opinion, in case the report of that mission should turn out as it did, that the recognition of the independence of that government would follow, as a matter of course. The surprise at a different course being pursued by the executive at the last session, was proportionably great. . . . Two years ago, he said, would, in his opinion, have been the proper time for recognising the independence of the south. Then the struggle was somewhat doubtful, and a kind office on the part of this government would have had a salutary effect. Since that period, what had occurred? Any thing to prevent a recognition of their independence, or to make it less expedient? No. . . .

What would I give, exclaimed he, could we appreciate the advantages which may be realized by pursuing the course which I propose! It is in our power to create a system of which we shall be the centre, and in which all South America will act with us. In respect to commerce, we shall be most benefited; this country would become the place of deposit of the commerce of the world. Our citizens engaged in foreign trade at present were disheartened by the condition of that trade; they must take new channels for it, and none so advantageous could be found, as those which the trade with South America would afford. Mr. Clay took a prospective view of the growth of wealth, and increase of population of this country and South America. That country had now a population of upwards of eighteen millions. The same activity in the principle of population would exist in that country as here. Twenty-five years hence it might be estimated at thirty-six millions; fifty years hence, at seventy-two millions. We now have a population of ten millions. From the character of our population, we must always take the lead in the prosecution of commerce and manufactures. Imagine the vast power of the two countries, and the value of the intercourse between them, when we shall have a population of forty millions, and they of seventy millions! In relation to South America, the people of the United States bear the same relation as the people of New England do to the rest of the United States.

Our enterprise, industry, and habits of economy, will give us the advantage in any competition which South America may sustain with us, and so forth.

But, however important our early recognition of the independence of the south might be to us, as respects our commercial and manufacturing interests, was there not another view of the subject, infinitely more gratifying? We should become the centre of a system which would constitute the rallying point of human freedom against all the despotism of the old world. Did any man doubt the feelings of the south towards us? In spite of our coldness towards them, of the rigor of our laws, and the conduct of our officers, their hearts still turned towards us, as to their brethren; and he had no earthly doubt, if our government would take the lead and recognise them, they would become yet more anxious to imitate our institutions, and to secure to themselves and to their posterity the same freedom which we enjoy.

On a subject of this sort, he asked, was it possible we could be content to remain, as we now were, looking anxiously to Europe . . .? Why not proceed to act on our own responsibility, and recognise these governments as independent, instead of taking the lead of the holy alliance in a course which jeopardizes the happiness of unborn millions. He deprecated this deference for foreign powers. . . . Our institutions now make us free; but how long shall we continue so, if we mould our opinions on those of Europe? Let us break these commercial and political fetters; let us no longer watch the nod of any European politician; let us become real and true Americans, and place ourselves at the head of the American system.

Gentlemen all said, they were all anxious to see the independence of the south established. If sympathy for them was enough, the patriots would have reason to be satisfied with the abundant expressions of it. But something more was wanting. Some gentlemen had intimated, that the people of the south were unfit for freedom. Will gentlemen contend, said Mr. Clay, because those people are not like us in all particulars, they are therefore unfit for freedom . . .?

With regard to the form of his proposition, all he wanted was, to obtain an expression of the opinion of the house on this subject; and whether a minister should be authorized to one or the other of these governments, or whether he should be of one grade or of another, he cared not. This republic, with the exception of the people of South America, constituted the sole depository of political and religious freedom; and can it be possible, said he, that we can remain passive spectators of the struggle of those people to break the same chains which once bound us? The opinions of the friends of freedom in Europe is, that our policy has been cold, heartless, and indifferent, towards the greatest cause which could possibly engage our affections and enlist our feelings in its behalf.

Mr. Clay concluded by saying that, whatever might be the decision of this house on this question, . . . he should there have the consolation of knowing that he had used *his* best exertions in favor of a people inhabiting a territory calculated to contain as many souls as the whole of Christendom besides, whose happiness was at stake, and which it was in the power of this government to do so much towards securing.

Wherever the standard of freedom and independence has been or shall be unfurled, there will her heart, her benedictions, and her prayers be. But she goes not abroad in search of monsters to destroy.
—JOHN QUINCY ADAMS, 1821.

*U*NTIL WITHIN A FEW DAYS preceding that which we have again assembled to commemorate, our fathers, the people of this union, had

Fourth of July Oration, 1821. *Niles' Weekly Register*, July 21, 1821.

constituted a portion of the British nation; a nation renowned in arts and arms, who, from a small island in the Atlantic ocean, had extended their dominion over considerable parts of every quarter of the globe. Governed themselves by a race of kings, whose title to sovereignty had originally been founded in *conquest*, spell-bound for a succession of ages under that portentous system of despotism and superstition which, in the name of the meek and humble Jesus, had been spread over the Christian world, the history of this nation had, for a period of seven hundred years, from the days of the conquest till our own, exhibited a conflict almost continual, between the oppressions of power and the claims of right. In the theories of the crown and the mitre, man had no rights. Neither the body nor the soul of the individual was his own. From the impenetrable gloom of this intellectual darkness, and the deep degradation of this servitude, the British nation had partially emerged. . . . The people of Britain, through long ages of civil war, had extorted from their tyrants, not *acknowledgments* but *grants*, of right. With this concession they had been content to stop in the progress of human improvement. They received their freedom as a donation from their sovereigns; they appealed for their privileges to a sign manual and a seal; they held their title to liberty, like their title to lands, from the bounty of a man. . . .

[The Declaration of Independence] was the first solemn declaration by a nation of the only *legitimate* foundation of civil government. It was the cornerstone of a new fabric, destined to cover the surface of the globe. It demolished, at a stroke, the lawfulness of all governments founded upon conquest. It swept away all the rubbish of accumulated centuries of servitude. It announced in practical form to the world the transcendent truth of the unalienable sovereignty of the people. It proved that the social compact was no figment of the imagination, but a real, solid, and sacred bond of the social union. From the day of this declaration the people of North America were no longer the fragment of a distant empire, imploring justice and mercy from an inexorable master in another hemisphere. They were no longer children appealing in vain to the sympathies of a heartless mother; no longer subjects leaning upon the shattered columns of royal promises, and invoking the faith of parchment to secure their rights. They were a nation, asserting as of right, and maintaining by war, its own existence. A nation was born in a day:

> How many ages hence
> Shall this lofty scene, be acted o'er
> In states unborn, and accents yet unknown.

It will be acted o'er . . ., but it can never be repeated. It stands, and must forever stand alone, a beacon on the summit of a mountain, to which all the inhabitants of the earth may turn their eyes for a genial and saving light, till time shall be lost in eternity, and this globe itself dissolve, nor leave a wreck behind. It stands forever, a light of admonition to the rulers of men, a light of salvation and redemption to the oppressed. So long as this planet shall be inhabited by human beings; so long as man shall be of social nature, so long as government shall be necessary to the great moral purposes of society: and so long as it shall be abused to the purposes of oppression, so long shall this declaration hold out to the sovereign and to the subject the extent and the boundaries of their respective rights and duties, founded in the laws of nature and nature's God. . . .

America, with the same voice which spoke herself into existence as a nation, proclaimed to mankind the inextinguishable rights of human nature, and the only lawful foundations of government. America, in the assembly of nations, since her admission among them, has invariably, though often fruitlessly, held forth to them the hand of honest friendship, of equal freedom, of generous reciprocity. She has uniformly spoken among them, though often to heedless and often to disdainful ears, the language of equal liberty, of equal justice, and of equal rights. She has, in the lapse of nearly half a century, without a single exception, respected the independence of other nations while asserting and maintaining her own. She has abstained from interference in the concerns of others, even when the conflict has been for principles to which she clings, as to the last vital drop that visits the heart. She has seen that probably for centuries to come, all the contests of that Aceldama, the European world, will be contests of inveterate power, and emerging right. Wherever the standard of freedom and independence has been or shall be unfurled, there will her heart, her benedictions, and her prayers be. But she goes not abroad in search of monsters to destroy. She is the well-wisher to the freedom and independence of all. She is the champion and vindicator only of her own. She will recommend the general cause by the countenance of her voice, and the benignant sympathy of her example. She well knows that by once enlisting under other banners than her own, were they even the banners of foreign independence, she would involve herself beyond the power of extrication, in all the wars of interest and intrigue, of individual avarice, envy, and ambition, which assume the colors and usurp the standard of freedom. The fundamental maxims of her policy would insensibly change from *liberty* to *force*. The frontlet upon her brow would no longer beam with the ineffable splendor of freedom and independence; but in its stead would soon be substituted an imperial diadem, flashing in false and tarnished lustre, the murky radiance of dominion and power. She might become the dictatress of the world. She would no longer be the ruler of her own spirit.

THE MONROE DOCTRINE

... With the Governments who have declared their independence and maintained it ... we could not view any interposition for the purpose of oppressing them, or controlling in any other manner their destiny, by any European power in any other light than as the manifestation of an unfriendly disposition toward the United States.

—JAMES MONROE, 1823.

THE CITIZENS OF the United States cherish sentiments the most friendly in favor of the liberty and happiness of their fellow-men on that side of the Atlantic. In the wars of the European powers in matters relating to themselves we have never taken any part, nor does it comport with our policy so to do. It is only when our rights are invaded or seriously menaced that we resent injuries or make preparation for our defense. With the movements in this hemisphere we are of necessity more immediately connected, and by causes which must be obvious to all enlightened and impartial observers. The political system of the allied powers is essentially different in this respect from that of America. This difference proceeds from that which exists in their respective Governments; and to the defense of our own, which has been achieved by the loss of so much blood and treasure, and matured by the wisdom of their most enlightened citizens, and under which we have enjoyed unexampled felicity, this whole nation is devoted. We owe it, therefore, to candor and to the

James Monroe, *The Monroe Doctrine*, December 2, 1823. Richardson, *op. cit.*, vol. II, pp. 218-219.

amicable relations existing between the United States and those powers to declare that we should consider any attempt on their part to extend their system to any portion of this hemisphere as dangerous to our peace and safety. With the existing colonies or dependencies of any European power we have not interfered and shall not interfere. But with the Governments who have declared their independence and maintained it, and whose independence we have, on great consideration and on just principles, acknowledged, we could not view any interposition for the purpose of oppressing them, or controlling in any other manner their destiny, by any European power in any other light than as the manifestation of an unfriendly disposition toward the United States. . . .

Our policy in regard to Europe, which was adopted at an early stage of the wars which have so long agitated that quarter of the globe, . . . remains the same, which is, not to interfere in the internal concerns of any of its powers; to consider the government *de facto* as the legitimate government for us; to cultivate friendly relations with it, and to preserve those relations by a frank, firm, and manly policy, meeting in all instances the just claims of every power, submitting to injuries from none. But in regard to those continents circumstances are eminently and conspicuously different. It is impossible that the allied powers should extend their political system to any portion of either continent without endangering our peace and happiness; nor can anyone believe that our southern brethren, if left to themselves, would adopt it of their own accord. It is equally impossible, therefore, that we should behold such interposition in any form with indifference. If we look to the comparative strength and resources of Spain and those new Governments, and their distance from each other, it must be obvious that she can never subdue them. It is still the true policy of the United States to leave the parties to themselves, in the hope that other powers will pursue the same course.

IV. Have-Not Nation

In the first four decades of the nineteenth century, Americans poured over the Appalachians into the fertile Mississippi valley, many crossing the boundaries dividing the United States from the Spanish Viceroyalty of New Spain and its successor, the Republic of Mexico. In 1836 American settlers in the Mexican province of Texas revolted against Mexico, established an independent republic, and petitioned for annexation to the United States. Owing to the fact that Texas tolerated Negro slavery, and that many Americans opposed any extension of slave territory, annexation did not come about until 1845. But then, when United States troops went into territory claimed by both Texas and Mexico, a war followed. American troops occupied a considerable part of Mexico, and in the end the United States acquired not only the Texas borderlands but also the areas that subsequently became New Mexico, Arizona, and California.

There is some evidence that President James K. Polk was motivated from the beginning by desire to obtain California, and that he deliberately brought on the war. Much of the public felt that the nation had a "manifest destiny" to expand westward. But, in the fashion that had become characteristically American, Polk defended his course not as one that would bring material advantages but as one that was morally right. His critics, among them a young Congressman from Illinois, Abraham Lincoln, disputed this contention.

In the progression from Jefferson and Hamilton to Clay and Adams to Polk and Lincoln, one can see the gradual crystallization of two primary criteria for a national policy: first, that it satisfy the conscience of Americans; second, that it appear morally right in the eyes of the world.

JAMES K. POLK AND

ABRAHAM LINCOLN ON

THE MERITS OF THE MEXICAN WAR

The United States never attempted to acquire Texas by conquest. On the contrary, at an early period after the people of Texas had achieved their independence they sought to be annexed to the United States.
—JAMES K. POLK, 1846.

THE EXISTING WAR with Mexico was neither desired nor provoked by the United States. On the contrary, all honorable means were resorted to to avert it. After years of endurance of aggravated and unredressed wrongs on our part, Mexico, in violation of solemn treaty stipulations and of every principle of justice recognized by civilized nations, commenced hostilities, and thus by her own act forced the war upon us. Long before the advance of our Army to the left bank of the Rio Grande we had ample cause of war against Mexico, and had the United States resorted to this extremity we might have appealed to the whole civilized world for the justice of our cause. I deem it to be my duty to present to you on the present occasion a condensed review of the injuries we had sustained, of the causes which led to the war, and of its progress since its commencement. This is rendered the more necessary because of the mis-

Annual Message, December 8, 1846. Richardson, *op. cit.*, vol. IV, pp. 472-488.

apprehensions which have to some extent prevailed as to its origin and true character. The war has been represented as unjust and unnecessary and as one of aggression on our part upon a weak and injured enemy. Such erroneous views, though entertained by but few, have been widely and extensively circulated, not only at home, but have been spread throughout Mexico and the whole world. A more effectual means could not have been devised to encourage the enemy and protract the war than to advocate and adhere to their cause, and thus give them "aid and comfort." It is a source of national pride and exultation that the great body of our people have thrown no such obstacles in the way of the Government in prosecuting the war successfully, but have shown themselves to be eminently patriotic and ready to vindicate their country's honor and interests at any sacrifice. The alacrity and promptness with which our volunteer forces rushed to the field on their country's call prove not only their patriotism, but their deep conviction that our cause is just.

The wrongs which we have suffered from Mexico almost ever since she became an independent power and the patient endurance with which we have borne them are without a parallel in the history of modern civilized nations. There is reason to believe that if these wrongs had been resented and resisted in the first instance the present war might have been avoided. One outrage, however, permitted to pass with impunity almost necessarily encouraged the perpetration of another, until at last Mexico seemed to attribute to weakness and indecision on our part a forbearance which was the offspring of magnanimity and of a sincere desire to preserve friendly relations with a sister republic.

Scarcely had Mexico achieved her independence, which the United States were the first among the nations to acknowledge, when she commenced the system of insult and spoliation which she has ever since pursued. Our citizens engaged in lawful commerce were imprisoned, their vessels seized, and our flag insulted in her ports. If money was wanted, the lawless seizure and confiscation of our merchant vessels and their cargoes was a ready resource, and if to accomplish their purposes it became necessary to imprison the owners, captains, and crews, it was done. Rulers superseded rulers in Mexico in rapid succession, but still there was no change in this system of depredation. The Government of the United States made repeated reclamations on behalf of its citizens, but these were answered by the perpetration of new outrages. Promises of redress made by Mexico in the most solemn forms were postponed or evaded. . . .

Had the United States . . . adopted compulsory measures and taken redress into their own hands, all our difficulties with Mexico would probably have been long since adjusted and the existing war have been averted. Magnanimity and moderation on our part only had the effect to complicate these difficulties and render an amicable settlement of them the more embarrassing. That such measures of redress under similiar provocations committed by any of the powerful nations of Europe would have been promptly resorted to by the United States can not be doubted. The national honor and the preservation of the national character throughout the world, as well as our own self-respect and the protection due to our own citizens, would have rendered such a resort indispensable. The history of no civilized nation in modern times has presented within so brief a period so many wanton attacks upon the honor of its flag and upon the property and persons of its citizens as had at that time been borne by the United States from the Mexican authorities and people. But Mexico was a sister republic on the North American continent, occupying a territory contiguous to our own, and was in a feeble and distracted condition, and these considerations, it is presumed, induced Congress to forbear still longer. . . .

Had the unlawful seizures of American property and the violation of the personal liberty of our citizens, to say nothing of the insults to our flag, which have occurred in the ports of Mexico taken place on the high seas, they would themselves long since have constituted a state of actual war between the two countries. In so long suffering Mexico to violate her most solemn treaty obligations, plunder our citizens of their property, and imprison their persons without affording them any redress we have failed to perform one of the first and highest duties which every government owes to its citizens, and the consequence has been that many of them have been reduced from a state of affluence to bankruptcy. The proud name of American citizen, which ought to protect all who bear it from insult and injury throughout the world, has afforded no such protection to our citizens in Mexico. We had ample cause of war against Mexico long before the breaking out of hostilities; but even then we forbore to take redress into our own hands until Mexico herself became the aggressor by invading our soil in hostile array and shedding the blood of our citizens.

Such are the grave causes of complaint on the part of the United States against Mexico—causes which existed long before the annexation of Texas to the American Union; and yet, animated by the love of peace and a magnanimous moderation, we did not adopt those measures of redress which under such circumstances are the justified resort of injured nations.

The annexation of Texas to the United States constituted no just cause of offense to Mexico. The pretext that it did so is wholly inconsistent and irreconcilable with well-authenticated facts connected with the revolution by which Texas became independent of Mexico. That this may be the more manifest, it may be proper to advert to the causes and to the history of the principal events of that revolution.

Texas constituted a portion of the ancient Province of Louisiana, ceded to the United States by France in the year 1803. In the year 1819 the United States, by the Florida treaty, ceded to Spain all that part of Louisiana within the present limits of Texas, and Mexico, by the revolution which separated her from Spain and rendered her an independent nation, succeeded to the rights of the mother country over this territory. In the year 1824 Mexico established a federal constitution, under which the Mexican Republic was composed of a number of sovereign States confederated together in a federal union similar to our own. Each of these States had its own executive, legislature, and judiciary, and for all except federal purposes was as independent of the General Government and that of the other States as is Pennsylvania or Virginia under our Constitution. Texas and Coahuila united and formed one of these Mexican States. The State constitution which they adopted, and which was approved by the Mexican Confederacy, asserted that they were "free and independent of the other Mexican United States and of every other power and dominion whatsoever," and proclaimed the great principle of human liberty that "the sovereignty of the state resides originally and essentially in the general mass of the individuals who compose it." To the Government under this constitution, as well as to that under the federal constitution, the people of Texas owed allegiance.

Emigrants from foreign countries, including the United States, were invited by the colonization laws of the State and of the Federal Government to settle in Texas. Advantageous terms were offered to induce them to leave their own country and become Mexican citizens. This invitation was accepted by many of our citizens in the full faith that in their new home they would be governed by laws enacted by representatives elected by themselves, and that their lives, liberty, and property would be protected by constitutional guaranties similar to those which existed in the Republic they had left. Under a Government thus organized they continued until the year 1835, when a military revolution broke out in the City of Mexico which entirely subverted the federal and State constitutions and placed a military dictator at the head of the Government. By a sweeping decree of a Congress subservient to the will of the Dictator the several State constitutions were abolished and the States themselves converted into mere departments of the central Government. The people of Texas were unwilling to submit to this usurpation. Resistance to such tyranny became a high duty. Texas was fully absolved from all allegiance to the central Government of Mexico from the moment that Government had abolished her State constitution and in its place substituted an arbitrary and despotic central government. Such were the principal causes of the Texan revolution. The people of Texas at once determined upon resistance and flew to arms. In the midst of

these important and exciting events, however, they did not omit to
place their liberties upon a secure and permanent foundation. They
elected members to a convention, who in the month of March, 1836,
issued a formal declaration that their "political connection with the
Mexican nation has forever ended, and that the people of Texas do
now constitute a *free, sovereign, and independent Republic,* and are
fully invested with all the rights and attributes which properly belong to independent nations." They also adopted for their government a liberal republican constitution. About the same time Santa
Anna, then the Dictator of Mexico, invaded Texas with a numerous
army for the purpose of subduing her people and enforcing obedi-
ence to his arbitrary and despotic Government. On the 21st of April,
1836, he was met by the Texan citizen soldiers, and on that day was
achieved by them the memorable victory of San Jacinto, by which
they conquered their independence. Considering the numbers engaged on the respective sides, history does not record a more brilliant
achievement. Santa Anna himself was among the captives.

In the month of May, 1836, Santa Anna acknowledged by a treaty
with the Texan authorities in the most solemn form "the full, entire,
and perfect independence of the Republic of Texas." It is true he was
then a prisoner of war, but it is equally true that he had failed to
reconquer Texas, and had met with signal defeat; that his authority
had not been revoked, and that by virtue of this treaty he obtained
his personal release. By it hostilities were suspended, and the army
which had invaded Texas under his command returned in pursuance
of this arrangement unmolested to Mexico.

From the day that the battle of San Jacinto was fought until the
present hour Mexico has never possessed the power to reconquer
Texas. . . .

Texas had been an independent state, with an organized government, defying the power of Mexico to overthrow or reconquer her,
for more than ten years before Mexico commenced the present war
against the United States. Texas had given such evidence to the world
of her ability to maintain her separate existence as an independent

nation that she had been formally recognized as such not only by the United States, but by several of the principal powers of Europe. These powers had entered into treaties of amity, commerce, and navigation with her. They had received and accredited her ministers and other diplomatic agents at their respective courts, and they had commissioned ministers and diplomatic agents on their part to the Government of Texas. If Mexico, notwithstanding all this and her utter inability to subdue or reconquer Texas, still stubbornly refused to recognize her as an independent nation, she was none the less so on that account. Mexico herself had been recognized as an independent nation by the United States and by other powers many years before Spain, of which before her revolution she had been a colony, would agree to recognize her as such; and yet Mexico was at that time in the estimation of the civilized world, and in fact, none the less an independent power because Spain still claimed her as a colony. If Spain had continued until the present period to assert that Mexico was one of her colonies in rebellion against her, this would not have made her so or changed the fact of her independent existence. Texas at the period of her annexation to the United States bore the same relation to Mexico that Mexico had borne to Spain for many years before Spain acknowledged her independence, with this important difference, that before the annexation of Texas to the United States was consummated Mexico herself, by a formal act of her Government, had acknowledged the independence of Texas as a nation. It is true that in the act of recognition she prescribed a condition which she had no power or authority to impose—that Texas should not annex herself to any other power—but this could not detract in any degree from the recognition which Mexico then made of her actual independence. Upon this plain statement of facts, it is absurd for Mexico to allege as a pretext for commencing hostilities against the United States that Texas is still a part of her territory.

But there are those who, conceding all this to be true, assume the ground that the true western boundary of Texas is the Nueces instead of the Rio Grande, and that therefore in marching our Army to the east bank of the latter river we passed the Texan line and invaded the territory of Mexico. A simple statement of facts known to exist will conclusively refute such an assumption. Texas, as ceded to the United States by France in 1803, has been always claimed as extending west to the Rio Grande or Rio Bravo. . . . Down to the conclusion of the Florida treaty, in February, 1819, by which this territory was ceded to Spain, the United States asserted and maintained their territorial rights to this extent. . . .

The Texas which was ceded to Spain by the Florida treaty of 1819 embraced all the country now claimed by the State of Texas between the Nueces and the Rio Grande. The Republic of Texas always claimed this river as her western boundary, and in her treaty made with Santa Anna in May, 1836, he recognized it as such. By the constitution which Texas adopted in March, 1836, passed "An act to define the boundaries of the Republic of Texas," in which they declared the Rio Grande from its mouth to its source to be their boundary, and by the said act they extended their "civil and political jurisdiction" over the country up to that boundary. During a period of more than nine years which intervened between the adoption of her constitution and her annexation as one of the States of our Union Texas asserted and exercised many acts of sovereignty and jurisdiction over the territory and inhabitants west of the Nueces. She organized and defined the limits of counties extending to the Rio Grande; she established courts of justice and extended her judicial system over the territory; she established a customhouse and collected duties, and also postoffices and post-roads, in it; she established a land office and issued numerous grants for land within its limits; a senator and a representative residing in it were elected to the Congress of the Republic and served as such before the act of annexation took place. In both the Congress and convention of Texas which gave their assent to the terms of annexation to the United States proposed by our Congress were representatives residing west of the Nueces, who took part in the act of annexation itself. This was the Texas which by the act of our Congress of the 29th of December, 1845, was admitted as one of the

States of our Union. That the Congress of the United States understood the State of Texas which they admitted into the Union to extend beyond the Nueces is apparent from the fact that on the 31st of December, 1845, only two days after the act of admission, they passed a law "to establish a collection district in the State of Texas," by which they created a port of delivery at Corpus Christi, situated west of the Nueces, and being the same point at which the Texas custom-house under the laws of that Republic had been located, and directed that a surveyor to collect the revenue should be appointed for that port by the President, by and with the advice and consent of the Senate. A surveyor was accordingly nominated, and confirmed by the Senate, and has been ever since in the performance of his duties. All these acts of the Republic of Texas and of our Congress preceded the orders for the advance of our Army to the east bank of the Rio Grande. Subsequently Congress passed an act "establishing certain post routes" extending west of the Nueces. The country west of that river now constitutes a part of one of the Congressional districts of Texas and is represented in the House of Representatives. The Senators from that State were chosen by a legislature in which the country west of that river was represented. In view of all these facts it is difficult to conceive upon what ground it can be maintained that in occupying the country west of the Nueces with our Army, with a view solely to its security and defense, we invaded the territory of Mexico. But it would have been still more difficult to justify the Executive, whose duty it is to see that the laws be faithfully executed, if in the face of all these proceedings, both of the Congress of Texas and of the United States, he had assumed the responsibility of yielding up the territory west of the Nueces to Mexico or of refusing to protect and defend this territory and its inhabitants, including Corpus Christi as well as the remainder of Texas, against the threatened Mexican invasion.

But Mexico herself has never placed the war which she has waged upon the ground that our Army occupied the intermediate territory between the Nueces and the Rio Grande. Her refuted pretension that

Texas was not in fact an independent state, but a rebellious province, was obstinately persevered in, and her avowed purpose in commencing a war with the United States was to reconquer Texas and to restore Mexican authority over the whole territory—not to the Nueces only, but to the Sabine. In view of the proclaimed menaces of Mexico to this effect, I deemed it my duty, as a measure of precaution and defense, to order our Army to occupy a position on our frontier as a military post, from which our troops could best resist and repel any attempted invasion which Mexico might make. Our Army had occupied a position at Corpus Christi, west of the Nueces, as early as August, 1845, without complaint from any quarter. Had the Nueces been regarded as the true western boundary of Texas, that boundary had been passed by our Army many months before it advanced to the eastern bank of the Rio Grande. In my annual message of December last I informed Congress that upon the invitation of both the Congress and convention of Texas I had deemed it proper to order a strong squadron to the coasts of Mexico and to concentrate an efficient military force on the western frontier of Texas to protect and defend the inhabitants against the menaced invasion of Mexico. In that message I informed Congress that the moment the terms of annexation offered by the United States were accepted by Texas the latter became so far a part of our own country as to make it our duty to afford such protection and defense, and that for that purpose our squadron had been ordered to the Gulf and our Army to take a "position between the Nueces and the Del Norte" or Rio Grande and to "repel any invasion of the Texan territory which might be attempted by the Mexican forces."

It was deemed proper to issue this order, because soon after the President of Texas, in April, 1845, had issued his proclamation convening the Congress of that Republic for the purpose of submitting to that body the terms of annexation proposed by the United States the Government of Mexico made serious threats of invading the Texan territory. These threats became more imposing as it became more apparent in the progress of the question that the people of Texas would decide in favor of accepting the terms of annexation, and finally they had assumed such a formidable character as induced both the Congress and convention of Texas to request that a military force should be sent by the United States into her territory for the purpose of protecting and defending her against the threatened invasion. It would have been a violation of good faith toward the people of Texas to have refused to afford the aid which they desired against a threatened invasion to which they had been exposed by their free determination to annex themselves to our Union in compliance with the overture made to them by the joint resolution of our Congress. Accordingly, a portion of the Army was ordered to advance into Texas. Corpus Christi was the position selected by General Taylor. He encamped at that place in August, 1845, and the Army remained in that position until the 11th of March, 1846, when it moved westward, and on the 28th of that month reached the east bank of the Rio Grande opposite to Matamoras. . . .

The movement of our Army to the Rio Grande was made by the commanding general under positive orders to abstain from all aggressive acts toward Mexico or Mexican citizens, and to regard the relations between the two countries as peaceful unless Mexico should declare war or commit acts of hostility indicative of a state of war, and these orders he faithfully executed. Whilst occupying his position on the east bank of the Rio Grande, within the limits of Texas, then recently admitted as one of the States of our Union, the commanding general of the Mexican forces, who, in pursuance of the orders of his Government, had collected a large army on the opposite shore of the Rio Grande, crossed the river, invaded our territory, and commenced hostilities by attacking our forces. Thus, after all the injuries which we had received and borne from Mexico, and after she had insultingly rejected a minister sent to her on a mission of peace, and whom she had solemnly agreed to receive, she consummated her long course of outrage against our country by commencing an offensive war and shedding the blood of our citizens on our own soil.

The United States never attempted to acquire Texas by conquest. On the contrary, at an early period after the people of Texas had achieved their independence they sought to be annexed to the United States. At a general election in September, 1836, they decided with great unanimity in favor of "annexation," and in November following the Congress of the Republic authorized the appointment of a minister to bear their request to this Government. This Government, however, having remained neutral between Texas and Mexico during the war between them, and considering it due to the honor of our country and our fair fame among the nations of the earth that we should not at this early period consent to annexation, nor until it should be manifest to the whole world that the reconquest of Texas by Mexico was impossible, refused to accede to the overtures made by Texas. On the 12th of April, 1844, after more than seven years had elapsed since Texas had established her independence, a treaty was concluded for the annexation of that Republic to the United States, which was rejected by the Senate. Finally, on the 1st of March, 1845, Congress passed a joint resolution for annexing her to the United States upon certain preliminary conditions to which her assent was required. The solemnities which characterized the deliberations and conduct of the Government and people of Texas on the deeply interesting questions presented by these resolutions are known to the world. The Congress, the Executive, and the people of Texas, in a convention elected for that purpose, accepted with great unanimity the proposed terms of annexation, and thus consummated on her part the great act of restoring to our Federal Union a vast territory which had been ceded to Spain by the Florida treaty more than a quarter of a century before.

After the joint resolution for the annexation of Texas to the United States had been passed by our Congress the Mexican minister at Washington addressed a note to the Secretary of State, bearing date on the 6th of March, 1845, protesting against it as "an act of aggression the most unjust which can be found recorded in the annals of modern history, namely, that of despoiling a friendly nation like

Mexico of a considerable portion of her territory," and protesting against the resolution of annexation as being an act "whereby the Province of Texas, as integral portion of the Mexican territory, is agreed and admitted into the American Union," and he announced that as a consequence his mission to the United States had terminated, and demanded his passports, which were granted. It was upon the absurd pretext, made by Mexico (herself indebted for her independence to a successful revolution), that the Republic of Texas still continued to be, notwithstanding all that had passed, a Province of Mexico that this step was taken by the Mexican minister.

Every honorable effort has been used by me to avoid the war which followed, but all have proved vain.

. . . I more than suspect . . . that he (President Polk) is deeply conscious of being in the wrong—that he feels the blood of this war, like the blood of Abel, is crying to Heaven against him.

—ABRAHAM LINCOLN, 1848.

Some, IF NOT ALL the gentlemen, on the other side of the House, who have addressed the committee within the last two days, have spoken rather complainingly, if I have rightly understood them, of the vote given a week or ten days ago, declaring that the war with Mexico was unnecessarily and unconstitutionally commenced by the President. I admit that such a vote should not be given, in mere party wantonness, and that the one given, is justly censurable, if it have no

Speech in the House of Representatives, January 12, 1848. (Lincoln's first speech in Congress). Roy P. Basler, Ed., *The Collected Works of Abraham Lincoln*. Rutgers University Press, New Brunswick, New Jersey, 1953, vol. I, pp. 431-440.

other, or better foundation. I am one of those who joined in that vote; and I did so under my best impression of the *truth* of the case. How I got this impression, and how it may possibly be removed, I will now try to show. When the war began, it was my opinion that all those who, because of knowing too *little*, or because of knowing too *much*, could not conscientiously approve the conduct of the President, in the beginning of it, should, nevertheless, as good citizens and patriots, remain silent on that point, at least till the war should be ended. Some leading democrats, including Ex President Van Buren, have taken this same view, as I understand them; and I adhered to it, and acted upon it, until since I took my seat here; and I think I should still adhere to it, were it not that the President and his friends will not allow it to be so. Besides the continual effort of the President to argue every silent vote given for supplies, into an endorsement of the justice and wisdom of his conduct—besides that singularly candid paragraph, in his late message in which he tells us that Congress, with great unanimity, only two in the Senate and fourteen in the House dissenting, had declared that, "by the act of the Republic of Mexico, a state of war exists between that Government and the United States," when the same journals that informed him of this, also informed him, that when that declaration stood disconnected from the question of supplies, sixty seven in the House, and not fourteen merely, voted against it—besides this open attempt to prove, by telling the *truth*, what he could not prove by telling the *whole truth* —demanding of all who will not submit to be misrepresented, in justice to themselves, to speak out—beside all this, one of my colleagues . . . at a very early day in the session brought in a set of resolutions, expressly endorsing the original justice of the war on the part of the President. Upon these resolutions, when they shall be put on their passage I shall be *compelled* to vote; so that I can not be silent, if I would. Seeing this, I went about preparing myself to give the vote understandingly when it should come. I carefully examined the President's messages, to ascertain what he himself had said and proved upon the point. The result of this examination was to make the impression, that taking for true, all the President states as facts, he falls far short of proving his justification; and that the President would have gone farther with his proof, if it had not been for the small matter, that the *truth* would not permit him. Under the impression thus made, I gave the vote before mentioned. I propose now to give, concisely, the process of the examination I made, and how I reached the conclusion I did. The President, in his first war message of May 1846, declares that the soil was *ours* on which hostilities were commenced by Mexico; and he repeats that declaration, almost in the same language, in each successive annual message, thus showing that he esteems that point, a highly essential one. In the importance of that point, I entirely agree with the President. To my judgment, it is the *very point*, upon which he should be justified, or condemned. In his message of Decr. 1846, it seems to have occurred to him, as is certainly true, that title—ownership—to soil, or any thing else, is not a simple fact; but is a conclusion following one or more simple facts; and that it was incumbent upon him, to present the facts, from which he concluded, the soil was ours, on which the first blood of the war was shed. . . .

The issue, as he presents it, is in these words, "But there are those who, conceding all this to be true, assume the ground that the true western boundary of Texas is the Nueces, instead of the Rio Grande; and that, therefore, in marching our army to the east bank of the latter river, we passed the Texan line, and invaded the territory of Mexico." Now this issue, is made up of two affirmatives and no negative. The main deception of it is, that it assumes as true, that *one* river or the *other* is necessarily the boundary; and cheats the superficial thinker entirely out of the idea, that *possibly* the boundary is somewhere *between* the two, and not actually at either. A further deception is, that it will let in *evidence*, which a true issue would exclude. A true issue, made by the President, would be about as follows, "I say, the soil *was ours*, on which the first blood was shed; there are those who say it was not."

I now proceed to examine the President's evidence, as applicable to such an issue. When that evidence is analyzed, it is all included in the following propositions:

1. That the Rio Grande was the Western boundary of Louisiana as we purchased it of France in 1803.

2. That the Republic of Texas always *claimed* the Rio Grande, as her Western boundary.

3. That by various acts, she had claimed it *on paper*.

4. That Santa Anna, in his treaty with Texas, recognised the Rio Grande, as her boundary.

5. That Texas *before,* and the U.S. *after,* annexation had *exercised* jurisdiction *beyond* the Nueces—*between* the two rivers.

6. That our Congress, *understood* the boundary of Texas to extend beyond the Nueces.

Now for each of these in its turn.

His first item is, that the Rio Grande was the Western boundary of Louisiana, as we purchased it of France in 1803; and seeming to expect this to be disputed, he argues over the amount of nearly a page, to prove it true; at the end of which he lets us know, that by the treaty of 1819, we sold to Spain the whole country from the Rio Grande eastward, to the Sabine. Now, admitting for the present, that the Rio Grande, was the boundary of Louisiana, what, under heaven, had that to do with the *present* boundary between us and Mexico? How, Mr. Chairman, the line, that once divided your land from mine, can *still* be the boundary between us, *after* I have sold my land to you, is, to me, beyond all comprehension. And how any man, with an honest purpose only, of proving the truth, could ever have *thought* of introducing such a fact to prove such an issue, is equally incomprehensible. His next piece of evidence is that "The Republic of Texas always *claimed* this river (Rio Grande) as her western boundary[.]" That is not true, in fact. Texas *has* claimed it, but she has not *always* claimed it. There is, at least, one distinguished exception. Her state constitution,—the republic's most solemn, and well considered act—that which may, without impropriety, be called her last will and testament revoking all others—makes no such claim. But suppose she had always claimed it. Has not Mexico always claimed the contrary? so that there is but *claim* against *claim,* leaving nothing proved, until we get back of the claims, and find which has the better *foundation.* Though not in the order in which the President presents his evidence, I now consider that class of his statements, which are, in substance, nothing more than that Texas has, by various acts of her convention and congress, claimed the Rio Grande, as her boundary, *on paper.* I mean here what he says about the fixing of the Rio Grande as her boundary in her old constitution (not her state constitution) about forming congressional districts, counties &c &c. Now all of this is but naked *claim;* and what I have already said about claims is strictly applicable to this. If I should claim your land, by word of mouth, that certainly would not make it mine; and if I were to claim it by a deed which I had made myself, and with which, you had had nothing to do, the claim would be quite the same, in substance—or rather, in utter nothingness. I next consider the President's statement that Santa Anna in his *treaty* with Texas, recognised the Rio Grande, as the western boundary of Texas. Besides the position, so often taken that Santa Anna, while a prisoner of war—a captive—*could* not bind Mexico by a treaty, which I deem conclusive—besides this, I wish to say something in relation to this treaty, so called by the President, with Santa Anna. If any man would like to be amused by a sight of that *little* thing, which the President calls by that *big* name, he can have it, by turning to Niles' Register volume 50, page 336. And if any one should suppose that Niles' Register is a curious repository of so mighty a document, as a solemn treaty between nations, I can only say that I learned, to a tolerable degree [of] certainty, by enquiry at the State Department, that the President himself, never saw it any where else. By the way, I believe I should not err, if I were to declare, that during the first ten years of the existence of that document, it was never, by any body, *called* a treaty—that it was never so called, till the President, in his extremity, attempted, by so calling it, to wring something from it in justification of himself in connection with the Mexican war. It has none of the distinguishing features of a treaty. It does not call itself a treaty. Santa Anna does not therein, assume to bind Mexico; he assumes only to act as the President-Commander-in-chief of the Mexican Army and Navy; stipulates that the then present hostilities should cease, and that he would not *himself* take up arms, nor *influence* the Mexican people to take up arms, against Texas during the existence of the war of independence[.] He did not recognise the independence of Texas; he did not assume to put an end to the war; but clearly indicated his expectation of its continuance; he did not say one word about boundary, and, most probably, never thought of it. It *is* stipulated therein that the Mexican forces should evacuate the territory of Texas, *passing to the other side of the Rio Grande;* and in another article, it is stipulated that, to prevent collisions between the armies, the Texan army should not approach nearer than within five leagues—of *what* is not said—but clearly, from the object stated it is—of the Rio Grande. Now, if this is a treaty, recognising the Rio Grande, as the boundary of Texas, it contains the singular feature, of stipulating, that Texas shall not go within five leagues of *her own* boundary.

Next comes the evidence of Texas before annexation, and the United States, afterwards, *exercising* jurisdiction *beyond* the Nueces, and *between* the two rivers. This actual *exercise* of jurisdiction, is the very class or quality of evidence we want. It is excellent so far as it goes; but does it go far enough? He tells us it went *beyond* the Nueces; but he does not tell us it went *to* the Rio Grande. He tells us, jurisdiction was exercised *between* the two rivers, but he does not tell us it was exercised over *all* the territory between them. Some simple minded people, think it is *possible,* to cross one river and go *beyond* it without going *all the way* to the next—that jurisdiction may be exercised *bewteen* two rivers without covering *all* the country between them. I know a man, not very unlike myself, who exercises jurisdiction over a piece of land between the Wabash and the Mississippi; and yet so far is this from being *all* there is between those rivers, that it is just one hundred and fifty two feet long by fifty wide, and no part of it much within a hundred miles of either. He has a neighbour between him and the Mississippi,—that is, just across the street, in that direction—whom, I am sure, he could neither *persuade* nor *force* to give up his habitation; but which nevertheless, he could certainly annex, if it were to be done, by merely standing on his own side of the street and *claiming* it, or even, sitting down, and writing a *deed* for it.

But next the President tells us, the Congress of the United States *understood* the state of Texas they admitted into the union, to extend *beyond* the Nueces. Well, I suppose they did. *I* certainly so understood it. But how *far* beyond? That Congress did *not* understand it to extend clear to the Rio Grande, is quite certain by the fact of their joint resolutions, for admission expressly leaving all questions of boundary to future adjustment. And it may be added, that Texas herself, is proved to have had the same understanding of it, that our Congress had, by the fact of the exact conformity of her new constitution, to those resolutions.

I am now through the whole of the President's evidence; and it is a singular fact, that if any one should declare the President sent the army into the midst of a settlement of Mexican people, who had never submitted, by consent or by force, to the authority of Texas or of the United States, and that *there*, and *thereby*, the first blood of the war was shed, there is not one word in all the President has said, which would either admit or deny the declaration. This strange omission, it does seem to me, could not have occurred but by design. My way of living leads me to be about the courts of justice; and there, I have sometimes seen a good lawyer, struggling for his client's neck, in a desperate case, employing every artifice to work round, befog, and cover up, with many words, some point arising in the case, which he *dared* not admit, and yet *could* not deny. Party bias may help to make it appear so; but with all the allowance I can make for such bias, it still does appear to me, that just such, and from just such necessity, is the President's struggle in this case.

Some time after my colleague . . . introduced the resolutions I have mentioned, I introduced a preamble, resolution, and interrogatories,

intended to draw the President out, if possible, on this hitherto un-
trodden ground. To show their relevancy, I propose to state my
understanding of the true rule for ascertaining the boundary between
Texas and Mexico. It is, that *wherever* Texas was *exercising* jurisdiction, was hers; and that *whatever* separated the actual exercise of
jurisdiction of the one, from that of the other, was the true boundary
between them. If, as is probably true, Texas was exercising jurisdiction along the western bank of the Nueces, and Mexico was exercising
it along the eastern bank of the Rio Grande, then *neither* river was
the boundary; but the uninhabited country between the two, was. The
extent of our territory in that region depended, not on any *treaty-
fixed* boundary (for no treaty had attempted it) but on revolution.
Any people anywhere, being inclined and having the power, have the
right to rise up, and shake off the existing government, and form a
new one that suits them better. This is a most valuable,—a most
sacred right—a right, which we hope and believe, is to liberate the
world. Nor is this right confined to cases in which the whole people
of an existing government, may choose to exercise it. Any portion of
such people that *can, may* revolutionize, and make their *own*, of so
much of the territory as they inhabit. More than this, a *majority* of
any portion of such people may revolutionize, putting down a *minority*, intermingled with, or near about them, who may oppose their
movement. Such minority, was precisely the case, of the tories of our
own revolution. It is a quality of revolutions not to go by *old* lines, or
old laws; but to break up both, and make new ones. As to the country
now in question, we bought it of France in 1803, and sold it to Spain
in 1819, according to the President's statements. After this, all
Mexico, including Texas, revolutionized against Spain; and still
later, Texas revolutionized against Mexico. In my view, just so far
as she carried her revolution, by obtaining the *actual*, willing or unwilling, submission of the people, *so far*, the country was hers, and no
farther. Now sir, for the purpose of obtaining the very best evidence,
as to whether Texas had actually carried her revolution to the place
where the hostilities of the present war commenced, let the President

answer the interrogatories I proposed, as before mentioned, or some other similar ones. Let him answer fully, fairly, and candidly. Let him answer with *facts*, and not with arguments. Let him remember he sits where Washington sat, and so remembering, let him answer, as Washington would answer. As a nation *should* not, and the Almighty *will* not, be evaded, so let him attempt no evasion—no equivocation. And if, so answering, he can show that the soil was ours, where the first blood of the war was shed—that it was not within an inhabited country, or, if within such, that the inhabitants had submitted themselves to the civil authority of Texas, or of the United States, . . . then I am with him for his justification. In that case I shall be most happy to reverse the vote I gave the other day. I have a selfish motive for desiring that the President may do this. I expect to give some votes, in connection with the war, which, without his so doing, will be of doubtful propriety in my own judgment, but which will be free from the doubt if he does so. But if he *can* not, or *will* not do this—if on any pretence, or no pretence, he shall refuse or omit it, then I shall be fully convinced of what I more than suspect already, that he is deeply conscious of being in the wrong—that he feels the blood of this war, like the blood of Abel, is crying to Heaven against him. That originally having some strong motive—what, I will not stop now to give my opinion concerning—to involve the two countries in a war, and trusting to escape scrutiny, by fixing the public gaze upon the exceeding brightness of military glory—that attractive rainbow, that rises in showers of blood—that serpent's eye, that charms to destroy—he plunged into it, and has swept, *on* and *on*, till, disappointed in his calculation of the ease with which Mexico might be subdued, he now finds himself, he knows not where.

V.   Nation Beset by Civil Strife

The dispute over slavery growing more and more bitter and parties forming, contrary to Washington's advice, along sectional lines, the nation in 1861 split into two warring camps, the Union and the Confederacy. The ensuing struggle, one of the most terrible and bloody in the history not only of America but of mankind, engrossed attention in other parts of the world. For a time, it seemed possible that England and one or more European states might take an active role, at least to the extent of recognizing the Southern Confederacy's independence.

Lincoln, president in the North, and Jefferson Davis, president in the South, carried on a continuous dialogue aimed at proving to their own people and to those of other nations the rightness of their respective causes. Since the issues between them were more profound than those between any other pair of antagonists in American history, their exchanges illuminate with remarkable clarity the extent to which all American thought about national policy had as its frame of reference the ideals summarized in the Declaration of Independence.

JEFFERSON DAVIS AND
ABRAHAM LINCOLN ON
THE ISSUES OF THE CIVIL WAR

Our present political position . . . illustrates the American idea that governments rest on the consent of the governed, and that it is the right of the people to alter or abolish them at will whenever they become destructive of the ends for which they were established.
                                    —JEFFERSON DAVIS, 1861.

CALLED TO THE DIFFICULT and responsible station of Chief Magistrate of the Provisional Government which you have instituted, I approach the discharge of the duties assigned to me with humble distrust of my abilities, but with a sustaining confidence in the wisdom of those who are to guide and aid me in the administration of public affairs, and in abiding faith in the virtue and patriotism of the people. . . . I enter upon the duties of the office to which I have been chosen with the hope that the beginning of our career, as a Confederacy, may not be obstructed by hostile opposition to our enjoyment of the separate existence and independence we have asserted, and which, with the blessing of Providence, we intend to maintain.

Our present political position has been achieved in a manner unprecedented in the history of nations. It illustrates the American idea that governments rest on the consent of the governed, and that it is the right of the people to alter or abolish them at will whenever they

Inaugural Address as President of the Provisional Confederate Government, February, 1861. Dunbar Rowland, Ed., *Jefferson Davis, Constitutionalist: His Letters, Papers, and Speeches*. Mississippi Department of Archives and History, Jackson, Mississippi, 1923, vol. V, pp. 49-51.

become destructive of the ends for which they were established. The declared purpose of the compact of the Union from which we have withdrawn was to "establish justice, insure domestic tranquillity, provide for the common defense, promote the general welfare, and secure the blessings of liberty to ourselves and our posterity;" and when, in the judgment of the sovereign States composing this Confederacy, it has been perverted from the purposes for which it was ordained, and ceased to answer the ends for which it was established, a peaceful appeal to the ballot box declared that, so far as they are concerned, the Government created by that compact should cease to exist. In this they merely asserted the right which the Declaration of Independence of July 4, 1776, defined to be "inalienable." Of the time and occasion of its exercise they as sovereigns were the final judges, each for itself. The impartial and enlightened verdict of mankind will vindicate the rectitude of our conduct; and He who knows the hearts of men will judge of the sincerity with which we have labored to preserve the Government of our fathers in its spirit.

The right solemnly proclaimed at the birth of the United States, and which has been solemnly affirmed and reaffirmed in the Bills of Rights of the States subsequently admitted into the Union of 1789, undeniably recognizes in the people the power to resume the authority delegated for the purposes of government. Thus the sovereign States here represented have proceeded to form this Confederacy; and it is by abuse of language that their act has been denominated a revolution. They formed a new alliance, but within each State its government has remained; so that the rights of person and property have not been disturbed. The agent through which they communicated with foreign nations is changed, but this does not necessarily interrupt their international relations. Sustained by the consciousness that the transition from the former Union to the present Confederacy has not proceeded from a disregard on our part of just obligations, or any failure to perform every constitutional duty, moved by no interest or passion to invade the rights of others, anxious to cultivate peace and commerce with all nations, if we may not hope to avoid war, we may

States was framed in 1787 and submitted to the *several States* for ratification. . . . The Constitution of 1787, having, however, omitted the clause . . . from the Articles of Confederation, which provided in explicit terms that each State *retained* its sovereignty and independence, some alarm was felt in the States, when invited to ratify the Constitution, lest this omission should be construed into an abandonment of their cherished principle, and they refused to be satisfied until amendments were added to the Constitution placing beyond any pretense of doubt the reservation by the States of all their sovereign rights and powers not expressly delegated to the United States by the Constitution.

Strange, indeed, must it appear to the impartial observer, but it is none the less true that all these carefully worded clauses proved unavailing to prevent the rise and growth in the Northern States of a political school which has persistently claimed that the government thus formed was not a compact *between* States, but was in effect a national government, set up *above* and *over* the States. An organization created by the States to secure the blessings of liberty and independence against *foreign* aggression, has been gradually perverted into a machine for their control in their *domestic* affairs. The *creature* has been exalted above its *creators;* the *principals* have been made subordinate to the *agent* appointed by themselves. . . . By degrees, as the Northern States gained preponderance in the National Congress, self-interest taught their people to yield ready assent to any plausible advocacy of their right as a majority to govern the minority without control. They learned to listen with impatience to the suggestion of any constitutional impediment to the exercise of their will, and so utterly have the principles of the Constitution been corrupted in the Northern mind that, in the inaugural address delivered by President Lincoln in March last, he asserts as an axiom, which he plainly deems to be undeniable, that the theory of the Constitution requires that in all cases the majority shall govern. . . . This is the lamentable and fundamental error on which rests the policy that has culminated in his declaration of war against these Confederate States. In addition to the long-continued and deep-seated resentment felt by the Southern States at the persistent abuse of the powers they had delegated to the Congress, for the purpose of enriching the manufacturing and shipping classes of the North at the expense of the South, there has existed for nearly half a century another subject of discord, involving interests of such transcendent magnitude as at all times to create the apprehension in the minds of many devoted lovers of the Union that its permanence was impossible. When the several States delegated certain powers to the United States Congress, a large portion of the laboring population consisted of African slaves imported into the colonies by the mother country. . . .

The climate and soil of the Northern States soon proved unpropitious to the continuance of slave labor, whilst the converse was the case at the South. Under the unrestricted free intercourse between the two sections, the Northern States consulted their own interests by selling their slaves to the South and prohibiting slavery within their limits. The South were willing purchasers of a property suitable to their wants, and paid the price of the acquisition without harboring a suspicion that their quiet possession was to be disturbed by those who were inhibited not only by want of constitutional authority, but by good faith as vendors, from disquieting a title emanating from themselves. As soon, however, as the Northern States that prohibited African slavery within their limits had reached a number sufficient to give their representation a controlling voice in the Congress, a persistent and organized system of hostile measures against the rights of the owners of slaves in the Southern States was inaugurated and gradually extended. A continuous series of measures was devised and prosecuted for the purpose of rendering insecure the tenure of property in slaves. Fanatical organizations, supplied with money by voluntary subscriptions, were assiduously engaged in exciting amongst the slaves a spirit of discontent and revolt; means were furnished for their escape from their owners, and agents secretly employed to entice them to abscond; the constitutional provision for their rendition to their owners was first evaded, then openly denounced as a violation of conscientious obligation and religious duty; men were taught that it was a merit to elude, disobey, and violently oppose the execution of the laws enacted to secure the performance of the promise contained in the constitutional compact; owners of slaves were mobbed and even murdered in open day solely for applying to a magistrate for the arrest of a fugitive slave. . . . Emboldened by success, the theater of agitation and aggression against the clearly expressed constitutional rights of the Southern States was transferred to the Congress; Senators and Representatives were sent to the common councils of the nation, whose chief title to this distinction consisted in the display of a spirit of ultra fanaticism, and whose business was not "to promote the general welfare or insure domestic tranquility," but to awaken the bitterest hatred against the citizens of sister States by violent denunciation of their institutions; the transaction of public affairs was impeded by repeated efforts to usurp powers not delegated by the Constitution, for the purpose of impairing the security of property in slaves, and reducing those States which held slaves to a condition of inferiority. Finally a great party was organized for the purpose of obtaining the administration of the Government, with the avowed object of using its power for the total exclusion of the slave States from all participation in the benefits of the public domain acquired by all the States in common, whether by conquest or purchase; of surrounding them entirely by States in which slavery should be prohibited; of thus rendering the property in slaves so insecure as to be comparatively worthless, and thereby annihilating in effect property worth thousands of millions of dollars. This party, thus organized, succeeded in the month of November last in the election of its candidate for the Presidency of the United States.

In the meantime, under the mild and genial climate of the Southern States and the increasing care and attention for the well-being and comfort of the laboring class, dictated alike by interest and humanity, the African slaves had augmented in number from about 600,000, at the date of the adoption of the constitutional compact, to upward of 4,000,000. In moral and social condition they had been elevated from brutal savages into docile, intelligent, and civilized agricultural laborers, and supplied not only with bodily comforts but with careful religious instruction. Under the supervision of a superior race their labor had been so directed as not only to allow a gradual and marked amelioration of their own condition, but to convert hundreds of thousands of square miles of the wilderness into cultivated lands covered with a prosperous people; towns and cities had sprung into existence, and had rapidly increased in wealth and population under the social system of the South; the white population of the Southern slaveholding States had augmented from about 1,250,000 at the date of the adoption of the Constitution to more than 8,500,000 in 1860; and the productions of the South in cotton, rice, sugar, and tobacco, for the full development and continuance of which the labor of African slaves was and is indispensable, had swollen to an amount which formed nearly three-fourths of the exports of the whole United States and had become absolutely necessary to the wants of civilized man. With interests of such overwhelming magnitude imperiled, the people of the Southern States were driven by the conduct of the North to the adoption of some course of action to avert the danger with which they were openly menaced. With this view the Legislatures of the several States invited the people to select delegates to conventions to be held for the purpose of determining for themselves what measures were best adopted to meet so alarming a crisis in their history. . . .

Having done this, they proceeded to form a new compact amongst themselves by new articles of confederation, which have been also ratified by the conventions of the several States with an approach to unanimity far exceeding that of the conventions which adopted the Constitution of 1787. They have organized their new Government in all its departments; the functions of the executive, legislative, and judicial magistrates are performed in accordance with the will of the people, as displayed not merely in a cheerful acquiescence, but in the enthusiastic support of the Government thus established by themselves; and but for the interference of the Government of the United States in this legitimate exercise of the right of a people to self-government, peace, happiness, and prosperity would now smile on our land.

The true character of the pretended new State is at once revealed. It is seen to be a Power in pronunciamento only.

—ABRAHAM LINCOLN AND
WILLIAM HENRY SEWARD, 1861.

*N*ow AFTER LONG FORBEARANCE, designed to soothe discontent and avert the need of civil war, the land and naval forces of the United States have been put in motion to repress the insurrection. The true character of the pretended new State is at once revealed. It is seen to be a Power existing in pronunciamento only. It has never won a field. It has obtained no forts that were not virtually betrayed into its hands or seized in breach of trust. It commands not a single port on the coast nor any highway out from its pretended Capital by Land. Under these circumstances Great Britain is called upon to intervene and give it body and independence by resisting our measures of suppression. British recognition would be British intervention to create within our own territory a hostile State by overthrowing this Republic itself. . . .

We are not insensible of the grave importance of this occasion. We see how upon the result of the debate in which we are engaged,

Instructions to Charles Francis Adams, United States Ambassador to Great Britain, May 21, 1861. Basler, *op. cit.,* vol. IV, pp. 379-380.

a war may ensue, between the United States and one, two, or even more European nations. War in any case is as exceptionable from the habits as it is revolting from the sentiments of the American people. But if it come it will be fully seen that it results from the action of Great Britain, not our own, that Great Britain will have decided to fraternize with our domestic enemy either without waiting to hear from you our remonstrances and our warnings or after having heard them. War in defence of national life is not immoral, and war in defence of independence is an inevitable part of the discipline of nations.

The dispute will be between the European and the American branches of the British race. All who belong to that race will especially deprecate it; as they ought. It may well be believed that men of every race and kindred will deplore it. A war not unlike it between the same parties occurred at the close of the last century. Europe atoned by forty years of suffering for the error that Great Britain committed in provoking that contest. If that nation shall now repeat the same great error, the social convulsions which will follow may not be so long but they will be more general. When they shall have ceased, it will, we think, be seen, whatever may have been the fortunes of other nations, that it is not the United States that will have come out of them with its precious constitution altered or its honestly obtained dominion in any degree abridged. Great Britain has but to wait a few months and all her present inconveniences will cease with all our own troubles. If she take a different course she will calculate for herself the ultimate as well as the immediate consequences, and will consider what position she will hold when she shall have forever lost the sympathies and the affections of the only nation on whose sympathies and affections she has a natural claim. In making that calculation she will do well to remember that in the controversy she proposes to open we shall be actuated by neither pride, nor passion, nor cupidity, nor ambition; but we shall stand simply on the principle of self preservation and that our cause will involve the independence of nations and the rights of human nature.

It continues to develop that the insurrection is largely, if not exclu-sively, a war upon the first principle of popular government—the rights of the people. —ABRAHAM LINCOLN, 1861.

A DISLOYAL PORTION of the American people have, during the whole year, been engaged in an attempt to divide and destroy the Union. A nation which endures factious domestic division, is exposed to disrespect abroad; and one party, if not both, is sure, sooner or later, to invoke foreign intervention.

Nations, thus tempted to interfere, are not always able to resist the counsels of seeming expediency, and ungenerous ambition, although measures adopted under such influences seldom fail to be unfortunate and injurious to those adopting them.

The disloyal citizens of the United States who have offered the ruin of our country, in return for the aid and comfort which they have invoked abroad, have received less patronage and encourage-ment than they probably expected. If it were just to suppose, as the insurgents have seemed to assume, that foreign nations, in this case, discarding all moral, social, and treaty obligations, would act solely, and selfishly, for the most speedy restoration of commerce, including, especially, the acquisition of cotton, those nations appear, as yet, not to have seen their way to their object more directly, or clearly, through the destruction, than through the preservation, of the Union. If we could dare to believe that foreign nations are actuated by no higher principle than this, I am quite sure a sound argument could be made to show them that they can reach their aim more readily, and easily, by aiding to crush this rebellion, than by giving encourage-ment to it.

The principal lever relied on by the insurgents for exciting foreign

Annual Message, December 3, 1861. Basler, *op. cit.*, vol. V, pp. 36-53.

nations to hostility against us, as already intimated, is the embarrassment of commerce. Those nations, however, not improbably, saw from the first, that it was the Union which made as well our foreign, as our domestic, commerce. They can scarcely have failed to perceive that the effort for disunion produces the existing difficulty; and that one strong nation promises more durable peace, and a more extensive, valuable and reliable commerce, than can the same nation broken into hostile fragments.

It is not my purpose to review our discussions with foreign states, because whatever might be their wishes, or dispositions, the integrity of our country, and the stability of our government, mainly depend, not upon them, but on the loyalty, virtue, patriotism, and intelligence of the American people. . . .

It continues to develop that the insurrection is largely, if not exclusively, a war upon the first principle of popular government—the rights of the people. Conclusive evidence of this is found in the most grave and maturely considered public documents, as well as in the general tone of the insurgents. In those documents we find the abridgement of the existing right of suffrage and the denial to the people of all right to participate in the selection of public officers, except the legislative, boldly advocated, with labored arguments to prove that large control of the people in government, is the source of all political evil. Monarchy itself is sometimes hinted at as a possible refuge from the power of the people.

In my present position, I could scarcely be justified were I to omit raising a warning voice against this approach of returning despotism.

It is not needed, nor fitting here, that a general argument should be made in favor of popular institutions; but there is one point, with its connexions, not so hackneyed as most others, to which I ask a brief attention. It is the effort to place *capital* on an equal footing with, if not above *labor*, in the structure of government. It is assumed that labor is available only in connexion with capital; that nobody labors unless somebody else, owning capital, somehow by the use of it, induces him to labor. This assumed, it is next considered whether it is best that capital shall *hire* laborers, and thus induce them to work by their own consent, or *buy* them, and drive them to it without their consent. Having proceeded so far, it is naturally concluded that all laborers are either *hired* laborers, or what we call slaves. And further it is assumed that whoever is once a hired laborer, is fixed in that condition for life.

Now, there is no such relation between capital and labor as assumed; nor is there any such thing as a free man being fixed for life in the condition of a hired laborer. Both these assumptions are false, and all inferences from them are groundless.

Labor is prior to, and independent of, capital. Capital is only the fruit of labor, and could never have existed if labor had not first existed. Labor is the superior of capital, and deserves much the higher consideration. Capital has its rights, which are as worthy of protection as any other rights. Nor is it denied that there is, and probably always will be, a relation between labor and capital, producing mutual benefits. The error is in assuming that the whole labor of community exists within that relation. A few men own capital, and that few avoid labor themselves, and, with their capital, hire or buy another few to labor for them. A large majority belong to neither class—neither work for others, nor have others working for them. In most of the southern States, a majority of the whole people of all colors are neither slaves nor masters; while in the northern a large majority are neither hirers nor hired. Men with their families—wives, sons, and daughters—work for themselves, on their farms, in their houses, and in their shops, taking the whole product to themselves, and asking no favors of capital on the one hand, nor of hired laborers or slaves on the other. It is not forgotten that a considerable number of persons mingle their own labor with capital—that is, they labor with their own hands, and also buy or hire others to labor for them; but this is only a mixed, and not a distinct class. No principle stated is disturbed by the existence of this mixed class.

Again: as has already been said, there is not, of necessity, any such thing as the free hired laborer being fixed to the condition for life. Many independent men everywhere in these States, a few years back in their lives, were hired laborers. The prudent, penniless beginner in the world, labors for wages awhile, saves a surplus with which to buy tools or land for himself; then labors on his own account another while, and at length hires another new beginner to help him. This is the just, and generous, and prosperous system, which opens the way to all—gives hope to all, and consequent energy, and progress, and improvement of condition to all. No men living are more worthy to be trusted than those who toil up from poverty—none less inclined to take, or touch, aught which they have not honestly earned. Let them beware of surrendering a political power which they already possess, and which, if surrendered, will surely be used to close the door of advancement against such as they, and to fix new disabilities and burdens upon them, till all of liberty shall be lost.

From the first taking of our national census to the last are seventy years; and we find our population at the end of the period eight times as great as it was at the beginning. The increase of those other things which men deem desirable has been even greater. We thus have at one view, what the popular principle applied to government, through the machinery of the States and the Union, has produced in a given time; and also what, if firmly maintained, it promises for the future. There are already among us those, who, if the Union be preserved, will live to see it contain two hundred and fifty millions. The struggle of today, is not altogether for today—it is for a vast future also. With a reliance on Providence, all the more firm and earnest, let us proceed in the great task which events have devolved upon us.

The tyranny of an unbridled majority, the most odious and least re-sponsible form of despotism, has denied us both the right and the remedy.   —JEFFERSON DAVIS, 1862.

THE FIRST YEAR in our history has been the most eventful in the annals of this continent. A new Government has been established, and its machinery put in operation over an area exceeding seven hundred thousand square miles. The great principles upon which we have been willing to hazard everything that is dear to man have made conquests for us which could never have been achieved by the sword. Our Confederacy has grown from six to thirteen States; and Mary-land, already united to us by hallowed memories and material inter-ests, will, I believe, when able to speak with unstifled voice, connect her destiny with the South. Our people have rallied with unexampled unanimity to the support of the great principles of constitutional gov-ernment, with firm resolve to perpetuate by arms the right which they could not peacefully secure. A million of men, it is estimated, are now standing in hostile array, and waging war along a frontier of thousands of miles. Battles have been fought, sieges have been conducted, and, although the contest is not ended, and the tide for the moment is against us, the final result in our favor is not doubtful.

The period is near at hand when our foes must sink under the im-mense load of debt which they have incurred, a debt which in their effort to subjugate us has already attained such fearful dimensions as will subject them to burdens which must continue to oppress them for generations to come.

We too have had our trials and difficulties. That we are to escape them in future is not to be hoped. It was to be expected when we

Inaugural Address as President of the Permanent Government of the Confederate States of America, February 22, 1862. Rowland, *op. cit.*, pp. 200-203.

entered upon this war that it would expose our people to sacrifices and cost them much, both of money and blood. But we knew the value of the object for which we struggled, and understood the nature of the war in which we were engaged. Nothing could be so bad as failure, and any sacrifice would be cheap as the price of success in such a contest.

But the picture has its lights as well as its shadows. This great strife has awakened in the people the highest emotions and qualities of the human soul. It is cultivating feelings of patriotism, virtue, and courage. Instances of self-sacrifice and of generous devotion to the noble cause for which we are contending are rife throughout the land. Never has a people evinced a more determined spirit than that now animating men, women, and children in every part of our country. Upon the first call the men flew to arms, and wives and mothers send their husbands and sons to battle without a murmur of regret.

It was, perhaps, in the ordination of Providence that we were to be taught the value of our liberties by the price which we pay for them.

The recollections of this great contest, with all its common traditions of glory, of sacrifice and blood, will be the bond of harmony and enduring affection amongst the people, producing unity in policy, fraternity in sentiment, and just effort in war.

Nor have the material sacrifices of the past year been made without some corresponding benefits. If the acquiescence of foreign nations in a pretended blockade has deprived us of our commerce with them, it is fast making us a self-supporting and an independent people. The blockade, if effectual and permanent, could only serve to divert our industry from the production of articles for export and employ it in supplying the commodities for domestic use.

It is a satisfaction that we have maintained the war by our unaided exertions. We have neither asked nor received assistance from any quarter. Yet the interest involved is not wholly our own. The world at large is concerned in opening our markets to its commerce. When the independence of the Confederate States is recognized by the nations of the earth, and we are free to follow our interests and in-clinations by cultivating foreign trade, the Southern States will offer to manufacturing nations the most favorable markets which ever in-vited their commerce. Cotton, sugar, rice, tobacco, provisions, timber, and naval stores will furnish attractive exchanges. Nor would the constancy of these supplies be likely to be disturbed by war. Our con-federate strength will be too great to tempt aggression; and never was there a people whose interests and principles committed them so fully to a peaceful policy as those of the Confederate States. By the character of their productions they are too keenly interested in foreign commerce wantonly to disturb it. War of conquest they cannot wage, because the Constitution of their Confederacy admits of no coerced association. Civil war there cannot be between States held together by their volition only. The rule of voluntary association, which cannot fail to be conservative, by securing just and impartial government at home, does not diminish the security of the obligations by which the Confederate States may be bound to foreign nations. In proof of this, it is to be remembered that, at the first moment of asserting their right to secession, these States proposed a settlement on the basis of the common liability for the obligations of the General Government.

Fellow-citizens, after the struggle of ages had consecrated the right of the Englishman to constitutional representative government, our colonial ancestors were forced to vindicate that birthright by an ap-peal to arms. Success crowned their efforts, and they provided for their posterity a peaceful remedy against future aggression.

The tyranny of an unbridled majority, the most odious and least responsible form of despotism, has denied us both the right and the remedy. Therefore we are in arms to renew such sacrifices as our fathers made to the holy cause of constitutional liberty. . . . With humble gratitude and adoration, acknowledging the Providence which has so visibly protected the Confederacy during its brief but eventful career, to thee, O God, I trustingly commit myself, and prayerfully invoke thy blessing on my country and its cause.

. . . One duty paramount to all others was before me, namely, to maintain and preserve at once the Constitution and the integrity of the federal republic.   —ABRAHAM LINCOLN, 1863.

**T*HE UNITED STATES have no enmities, animosities, or rivalries, and no interests which conflict with the welfare, safety and rights or interests of any other nation. Their own prosperity, happiness and aggrandizement are sought most safely and advantageously through the preservation, not only of peace on their own part, but peace among all other nations. But while the United States are thus a friend to all other nations, they do not seek to conceal the fact that they cherish especial sentiments of friendship for, and sympathies with, those who, like themselves, have founded their institutions on the principle of the equal rights of men; and such nations, being more prominently neighbors of the United States, the latter are co-operating with them in establishing civilization and culture on the American continent.

**I have the honor to acknowledge the receipt of the address and resolutions which you sent to me on the eve of the new year.

When I came, on the fourth day of March, 1861, through a free and constitutional election, to preside in the government of the United States, the country was found at the verge of civil war. Whatever might have been the cause, or whosoever the fault, one duty paramount to all others was before me, namely, to maintain and preserve at once the Constitution and the integrity of the federal repub-

* Letter to Frederico Barreda, Peruvian Minister to the United States, March 4, 1862. Basler, *op. cit.*, vol. V, pp. 142-143.
** Letter to the Workingmen of Manchester, England, January 19, 1863. Basler, *op. cit.*, vol. VI, pp. 63-65.

lic. A conscientious purpose to perform this duty is a key to all the measures of administration which have been, and to all which will hereafter be pursued. Under our form of government, and my official oath, I could not depart from this purpose if I would. It is not always in the power of governments to enlarge or restrict the scope of moral results which follow the policies that they may deem it necessary for the public safety, from time to time, to adopt.

I have understood well that the duty of self-preservation rests solely with the American people. But I have at the same time been aware that favor or disfavor of foreign nations might have a material influence in enlarging and prolonging the struggle with disloyal men in which the country is engaged. A fair examination of history has seemed to authorize a belief that the past action and influences of the United States were generally regarded as having been beneficent towards mankind. I have therefore reckoned upon the forbearance of nations. Circumstances, to some of which you kindly allude, induced me especially to expect that if justice and good faith should be practiced by the United States, they would encounter no hostile influence on the part of Great Britain. It is now a pleasant duty to acknowledge the demonstration you have given of your desire that a spirit of peace and amity towards this country may prevail in the councils of your Queen, who is respected and esteemed in your own country only more than she is by the kindred nation which has its home on this side of the Atlantic.

I know and deeply deplore the sufferings which the workingmen at Manchester and in all Europe are called to endure in this crisis. It has been often and studiously represented that the attempt to overthrow this government, which was built upon the foundation of human rights, and to substitute for it one which should rest exclusively on the basis of human slavery, was likely to obtain the favor of Europe. Through the actions of our disloyal citizens the workingmen of Europe have been subjected to a severe trial, for the purpose of forcing their sanction to that attempt. Under these circumstances, I cannot but regard your decisive utterance upon the question as an instance of sublime Christian heroism which has not been surpassed in any age or in any country. It is, indeed, an energetic and reinspiring assurance of the inherent power of truth and of the ultimate and universal triumph of justice, humanity, and freedom. I do not doubt that the sentiments you have expressed will be sustained by your great nation, and, on the other hand, I have no hesitation in assuring you that they will excite admiration, esteem, and the most reciprocal feelings of friendship among the American people. I hail this interchange of sentiment, therefore, as an augury that, whatever else may happen, whatever misfortune may befall your country or my own, the peace and friendship which now exist between the two nations will be, as it shall be my desire to make them, perpetual.

They sought to infringe upon the rights we had; and we only instituted a new government on the basis of those rights. . . .
                                                    —JEFFERSON DAVIS, 1864.

WE COMMENCED the fight without an army, without a navy, without arsenals, without mechanics, without money and without credit. Four years we have stemmed the tide of invasion, and to-day are stronger than when the war began; better able now than ever to repulse the vandal who is seeking our overthrow. Once we imported the commonest articles of daily use, and brought in from beyond our borders even bread and meat. Now the State of Georgia alone produces food enough not only for her own people and the army within it, but feeds, too, the Army of Virginia. Once we had no arms, and could receive no soldiers but those who came to us armed. Now we

Speech at Augusta, Georgia, October 10, 1864. Rowland, *op. cit.*, vol. VI, pp. 357-359.

have arms for all, and are begging men to bear them. This city of Augusta alone produces more power than the army can burn. All things are fair; and this Confederacy is not yet, in the familiar parlance of the croaker, "played out," as those declare who spread their own despondency over the whole body politic. (Voice in the crowd, beyond doubt that of a Hibernian, "Three cheers for the Confederacy," which were vociferously given.)

From the accents of that voice, my friend, I see that you have come into this country from one that has itself lost its liberty, and you may well exclaim three cheers for the Confederacy, upon whose success now alone depends the existence of constitutional liberty in the world—We are fighting for that principle—upon us depends its last hope. The Yankees, in endeavoring to coerce the States, have lost that heirloom of their fathers, and the men of the South alone must sustain it.

Ours is not a revolution. We are a free and independent people, in States that had the right to make a better government when they saw fit. They sought to infringe upon the rights we had; and we only instituted a new government on the basis of those rights. We are not engaged in a Quixotic fight for the rights of man; our struggle is for inherited rights; and who would surrender them? Let every paper guaranty possible be given, and who would submit?—From the grave of many a fallen hero the blood of the slain would cry out against such a peace with the murderers. . . .

Who now looks for intervention? Who does not know that our friends abroad depend upon our strength at home? That the balance is in our favor with victory, and turns against us with defeat, and that when our victory is unquestioned we will be recognized, and not till then. . . .

We will achieve it. How many sacrifices it may take, I cannot tell; but I believe that a just God looks upon our cause as holy, and that of our enemy as iniquitous. He may chastise us for our offences, but in so doing He is preparing us, and in His good Providence will assist us, and never desert the right.

VI.   Colonial Power

After the Union's triumph in the Civil War, the United States experienced a marvelous surge of economic and industrial growth. By the last years of the century, it had grown to such a point as to be clearly one of the great powers of the globe, and the issue that had arisen between Clay and John Quincy Adams came to the fore again: Should the nation seek actively to impose its will, ideals, and political system on peoples in one part of the world, or strive to set an example, hoping thereby eventually to make converts of all nations?

Events forced discussion of the issue. In the late 1890's Cuba, the last of Spain's colonies in the Americas, became the scene of a war for independence. After it raged for three bloody years, the sympathies of Americans became uncontainable. War was declared against Spain, and fighting that lasted just three months left the United States mistress of almost all the Spanish overseas colonies—Cuba, Puerto Rico, and the Philippine Islands. The former it was sworn to make independent; the latter two, however, President William McKinley decided to keep.

Some Americans were enthusiastic about such "imperialism." Others were not. Theodore Roosevelt took up the cause that, in a different way, Clay had championed three-quarters of a century earlier, while William Jennings Bryan spoke for the alternative—the policy of which Adams had been the champion in the 1820's.

THEODORE ROOSEVELT AND

WILLIAM JENNINGS BRYAN ON

AMERICA'S MISSION IN THE WORLD

If we are to be a really great people, we must strive in good faith to play a great part in the world. . . . The twentieth century looms before us big with the fate of many nations.
                    —THEODORE ROOSEVELT, 1899.

I WISH TO PREACH, not the doctrine of ignoble ease, but the doctrine of the strenuous life, the life of toil and effort, of labor and strife; to preach that highest form of success which comes, not to the man who desires mere easy peace, but to the man who does not shrink from danger, from hardship, or from bitter toil, and who out of these wins the splendid ultimate triumph.

A life of slothful ease, a life of that peace which springs merely from lack either of desire or of power to strive after great things, is as little worthy of a nation as of an individual. I ask only that what every self-respecting American demands from himself and from his sons shall be demanded of the American nation as a whole. Who among you would teach your boys that ease, that peace, is to be the first consideration in their eyes—to be the ultimate goal after which they strive . . .?

Theodore Roosevelt, *The Strenuous Life.* The Century Company, New York, 1899, pp. 319-331.

In the last analysis a healthy state can exist only when the men and women who make it up lead clean, vigorous, healthy lives; when the children are so trained that they shall endeavor, not to shirk difficulties, but to overcome them; not to seek ease, but to know how to wrest triumph from toil and risk. The man must be glad to do a man's work, to dare and endure and to labor; to keep himself, and to keep those dependent upon him. The woman must be the housewife, the helpmeet of the homemaker, the wise and fearless mother of many healthy children. In one of Daudet's powerful and melancholy books he speaks of "the fear of maternity, the haunting terror of the young wife of the present day." When such words can be truthfully written of a nation, that nation is rotten to the heart's core. When men fear work or fear righteous war, when women fear motherhood, they tremble on the brink of doom; and well it is that they should vanish from the earth, where they are fit subjects for the scorn of all men and women who are themselves strong and brave and high-minded.

As it is with the individual, so it is with the nation. It is a base untruth to say that happy is the nation that has no history. Thrice happy is the nation that has a glorious history. Far better it is to dare mighty things, to win glorious triumphs, even though checkered by failure, than to take rank with those poor spirits who neither enjoy much nor suffer much, because they live in the gray twilight that knows not victory nor defeat. If in 1861 the men who loved the Union had believed that peace was the end of all things, and war and strife the worst of all things, and had acted up to their belief, we would have saved hundreds of thousands of lives, we would have saved hundreds of millions of dollars. Moreover, besides saving all the blood and treasure we then lavished, we would have prevented the heartbreak of many women, the dissolution of many homes, and we would have spared the country those months of gloom and shame when it seemed as if our armies marched only to defeat. We could have avoided all this suffering simply by shrinking from strife. And if we had thus avoided it, we would have shown that we were weaklings, and that we were unfit to stand among the great nations of the earth. . . .

We of this generation do not have to face a task such as that our fathers faced, but we have our tasks, and woe to us if we fail to perform them! We cannot, if we would, play the part of China, and be content to rot by inches in ignoble ease within our borders, taking no interest in what goes on beyond them, sunk in a scrambling commercialism; heedless of the higher life, the life of aspiration, of toil and risk; busying ourselves only with the wants of our bodies for the day, until suddenly we should find, beyond a shadow of question, what China has already found, that in this world the nation that has trained itself to a career of unwarlike and isolated ease is bound, in the end, to go down before other nations which have not lost the manly and adventurous qualities. If we are to be a really great people, we must strive in good faith to play a great part in the world. We cannot avoid meeting great issues. All that we can determine for ourselves is whether we shall meet them well or ill. In 1898 we could not help being brought face to face with the problem of war with Spain. All we could decide was whether we should shrink like cowards from the contest, or enter into it as beseemed a brave and high-spirited people; and, once in, whether failure or success should crown our banners. So it is now. We cannot avoid the responsibilities that confront us in Hawaii, Cuba, Porto Rico, and the Philippines. All we can decide is whether we shall meet them in a way that will redound to the national credit, or whether we shall make of our dealings with these new problems a dark and shameful page in our history. To refuse to deal with them at all merely amounts to dealing with them badly. We have a given problem to solve. If we undertake the solution, there is, of course, always danger that we may not solve it aright; but to refuse to undertake the solution simply renders it certain that we cannot possibly solve it aright. The timid man, the lazy man, the man who distrusts his country, the over-civilized man, who has lost the great fighting, masterful virtues, the ignorant man, and the man of dull mind, whose soul is incapable of feeling the mighty lift that thrills "stern men with empires in their brains"—all these, of course, shrink from seeing the nation undertake its new duties; shrink from seeing us build a navy and an army adequate to our needs; shrink from seeing us do our share of the world's work, by bringing order out of chaos in the great, fair tropic islands from which the valor of our soldiers and sailors has driven the Spanish flag. These are the men who fear the strenuous life, who fear the only national life which is really worth leading. . . .

We cannot sit huddled within our own borders and avow ourselves merely an assemblage of well-to-do hucksters who care nothing for what happens beyond. Such a policy would defeat even its own end; for as the nations grow to have ever wider and wider interests, and are brought into closer and closer contact, if we are to hold our own in the struggle for naval and commercial supremacy, we must build up our power without our own borders. We must . . . grasp the points of vantage which will enable us to have our say in deciding the destiny of the oceans of the East and the West.

So much for the commercial side. From the standpoint of international honor the argument is even stronger. The guns that thundered off Manila and Santiago left us echoes of glory, but they also left us a legacy of duty. If we drove out a mediaeval tyranny only to make room for savage anarchy, we had better not have begun the task at all. It is worse than idle to say that we have no duty to perform, and can leave to their fates the islands we have conquered. Such a course would be the course of infamy. It would be followed at once by utter chaos in the wretched islands themselves. Some stronger, manlier power would have to step in and do the work, and we would have shown ourselves weaklings, unable to carry to successful completion the labors that great and high-spirited nations are eager to undertake.

The work must be done; we cannot escape our responsibility; and if we are worth our salt, we shall be glad of the chance to do the work —glad of the chance to show ourselves equal to one of the great tasks set modern civilization. But let us not deceive ourselves as to the importance of the task. Let us not be misled by vainglory into underestimating the strain it will put on our powers. . . .

Our proper conduct toward the tropic islands we have wrested from Spain is merely the form which our duty has taken at the moment. Of course we are bound to handle the affairs of our own household well. We must see that there is civic honesty, civic cleanliness, civic good sense in our home administration of city, State, and nation. We must strive for honesty in office, for honesty toward the creditors of the nation and of the individual; for the widest freedom of individual initiative where possible, and for the wisest control of individual initiative where it is hostile to the welfare of the many. But because we set our own household in order we are not thereby excused from playing our part in the great affairs of the world. A man's first duty is to his own home, but he is not thereby excused from doing his duty to the State; for if he fails in this second duty it is under the penalty of ceasing to be a free-man. In the same way, while a nation's first duty is within its own borders, it is not thereby absolved from facing its duties in the world as a whole; and if it refuses to do so, it merely forfeits its right to struggle for a place among the peoples that shape the destiny of mankind.

In the West Indies and the Philippines alike we are confronted by most difficult problems. It is cowardly to shrink from solving them in the proper way; for solved they must be, if not by us, then by some stronger and more manful race. If we are too weak, too selfish, or too foolish to solve them, some bolder and abler people must undertake the solution. Personally, I am far too firm a believer in the greatness of my country and the power of my countrymen to admit for one moment that we shall ever be driven to the ignoble alternative.

The problems are different for the different islands. Porto Rico is not large enough to stand alone. We must govern it wisely and well, primarily in the interest of its own people. Cuba is, in my judgment, entitled ultimately to settle for itself whether it shall be an independent state or an integral portion of the mightiest of republics. But until order and stable liberty are secured, we must remain in the island to insure them, and infinite tact, judgment, moderation, and courage must be shown by our military and civil representatives in keeping the island pacified, in relentlessly stamping out brigandage, in protecting all alike, and yet in showing proper recognition to the men who have fought for Cuban liberty. The Philippines offer a yet graver problem. . . . Many of their people are utterly unfit for self-government, and show no signs of becoming fit. Others may in time become fit but at present can only take part in self-government under a wise supervision, at once firm and beneficent. We have driven Spanish tyranny from the islands. If we now let it be replaced by savage anarchy, our work has been for harm and not for good. I have scant patience with those who fear to undertake the task of governing the Philippines, and who openly avow that they do fear to undertake it, or that they shrink from it because of the expense and trouble; but I have even scanter patience with those who make a pretense of humanitarianism to hide and cover their timidity, and who cant about "liberty" and the "consent of the governed," in order to excuse themselves for their unwillingness to play the part of men. Their doctrines, if carried out, would make it incumbent upon us to leave the Apaches of Arizona to work out their own salvation, and to decline to interfere in a single Indian reservation. Their doctrines condemn your forefathers and mine for ever having settled in these United States.

England's rule in India and Egypt has been of great benefit to England, for it has trained up generations of men accustomed to look at the larger and loftier side of public life. It has been of even greater benefit to India and Egypt. And finally, and most of all, it has advanced the cause of civilization. So, if we do our duty aright in the Philippines, we will add to that national renown which is the highest and finest part of national life, will greatly benefit the people of the Philippine Islands, and, above all, we will play our part well in the great work of uplifting mankind. But to do this work, keep ever in mind that we must show in a very high degree the qualities of courage, of honesty, and of good judgment. Resistance must be stamped out. The first and all-important work to be done is to establish the supremacy of our flag. We must put down armed resistance before we can accomplish anything else, and there should be no parleying, no faltering, in dealing with our foe. . . .

When once we have put down armed resistance, when once our rule is acknowledged, then an even more difficult task will begin, for then we must see to it that the islands are administered with absolute honesty and with good judgment. If we let the public service of the islands be turned into the prey of the spoils politician, we shall have begun to tread the path which Spain trod to her own destruction. We must send out there only good and able men, chosen for their fitness, and not because of their partizan service, and these men must not only administer impartial justice to the natives and serve their own government with honesty and fidelity, but must show the utmost tact and firmness, remembering that, with such people as those with whom we are to deal, weakness is the greatest of crimes, and that next to weakness comes lack of consideration for their principles and prejudices.

I preach to you, then, my countrymen, that our country calls not for the life of ease but for the life of strenuous endeavor. The twentieth century looms before us big with the fate of many nations. If we stand idly by, if we seek merely swollen, slothful ease and ignoble peace, if we shrink from the hard contests where men must win at hazard of their lives and at the risk of all they hold dear, then the bolder and stronger peoples will pass us by, and will win for themselves the domination of the world. Let us therefore boldly face the life of strife, resolute to do our duty well and manfully; resolute to uphold righteousness by deed and by word; resolute to be both honest and brave, to serve high ideals, yet to use practical methods. Above all, let us shrink from no strife, moral or physical, within or without the nation, provided we are certain that the strife is justified, for it is only through strife, through hard and dangerous endeavor, that we shall ultimately win the goal of true national greatness.

Those who would have this Nation enter upon a career of empires must consider, not only the effect of imperialism on the Filipinos, but they must also calculate its effects upon our own nation.

—WILLIAM JENNINGS BRYAN, 1900.

Speech accepting the Democratic Nomination for the Presidency, August 8, 1900. *Speeches of William Jennings Bryan.* Funk and Wagnalls, New York, 1909, pp. 24-49.

SOME ONE HAS SAID that a truth once spoken can never be recalled. It goes on and on, and no one can set a limit to its ever-widening influence. But if it were possible to obliterate every word written or spoken in defense of the principles set forth in the Declaration of Independence, a war of conquest would still leave its legacy of perpetual hatred, for it was God himself who placed in every human heart the love of liberty. He never made a race of people so low in the scale of civilization or intelligence that it would welcome a foreign master.

Those who would have this Nation enter upon a career of empires must consider, not only the effect of imperialism on the Filipinos, but they must also calculate its effects upon our own nation. We cannot repudiate the principle of self-government in the Philippines without weakening that principle here.

Lincoln said that the safety of this Nation was not in its fleets, its armies, or its forts, but in the spirit which prizes liberty as the heritage of all men, in all lands, everywhere, and he warned his countrymen that they could not destroy this spirit without planting the seeds of despotism at their own doors.

Even now we are beginning to see the paralyzing influence of imperialism. Heretofore this Nation has been prompt to express its sympathy with those who were fighting for civil liberty. While our sphere of activity has been limited to the Western Hemisphere, our sympathies have not been bounded by the seas. We have felt it due to ourselves and to the world, as well as to those who were struggling for the right to govern themselves, to proclaim the interest which our people have, from the date of their own independence, felt in every contest between human rights and arbitrary power.

Three-quarters of a century ago, when our nation was small, the struggles of Greece aroused our people, and Webster and Clay gave eloquent expression to the universal desire for Grecian independence. In 1898 all parties manifested a lively interest in the success of the Cubans, but now when a war is in progress in South Africa, which must result in the extension of the monarchical idea, or in the triumph of a republic, the advocates of imperialism in this country dare not say a word in behalf of the Boers. . . .

If this nation surrenders its belief in the universal application of the principles set forth in the Declaration of Independence, it will lose the prestige and influence which it has enjoyed among the nations as an exponent of popular government. . . .

A colonial policy means that we shall send to the Philippine Islands a few traders, a few taskmasters and a few office-holders and an army large enough to support the authority of a small fraction of the people while they rule the natives.

If we have an imperial policy we must have a great standing army as its natural and necessary complement. The spirit which will justify the forcible annexation of the Philippine Islands will justify the seizure of other islands and the domination of other people, and with wars of conquest we can expect a certain, if not rapid, growth of our military establishment. . . .

A large standing army is not only a pecuniary burden to the people and, if accompanied by compulsory service, a constant source of irritation, but it is ever a menace to a republican form of government.

The army is the personification of force and militarism will inevitably change the ideals of the people and turn the thoughts of our young men from the arts of peace to the science of war. The government which relies for its defense upon its citizens is more likely to be just than one which has at call a large body of professional soldiers. . . .

The Republican platform says that "the largest measure of self-government consistent with their welfare and our duties shall be secured to them (the Filipinos) by law." This is a strange doctrine for a government which owes its very existence to the men who offered their lives as a protest against government without consent and taxation without representation.

In what respect does the position of the Republican party differ from the position taken by the English government in 1776? Did not the English government promise a good government to the colonists? What king ever promised a bad government to his people? Did not the English government promise that the colonists should have the largest measure of self-government consistent with their welfare and English duties? Did not the Spanish government promise to give to the Cubans the largest measure of self-government consistent with their welfare and Spanish duties? The whole difference between a monarchy and a republic may be summed up in one sentence. In a monarchy the king gives to the people what he believes to be a good government; in a republic the people secure for themselves what they believe to be a good government.

The Republican party has accepted the European idea and planted itself upon the ground taken by George III, and by every ruler who distrusts the capacity of the people for self-government or denies them a voice in their own affairs. . . .

Is the sunlight of full citizenship to be enjoyed by the people of the United States, and the twilight of semi-citizenship endured by the people of Porto Rico, while the thick darkness of perpetual vassalage covers the Philippines . . .?

The Democratic party disputes this doctrine and denounces it as repugnant to both the letter and spirit of our organic law. There is no place in our system of government for the deposit of arbitrary and irresponsible power. That the leaders of a great party should claim for any President or Congress the right to treat millions of people as mere "possessions" and deal with them unrestrained by the Constitution or the bill of rights shows how far we have already departed from the ancient landmarks and indicates what may be expected if this nation deliberately enters upon a career of empire. . . .

Let us consider briefly the reasons which have been given in support of an imperialistic policy. Some say that it is our duty to hold the Philippine Islands. But duty is not an argument; it is a conclusion. To ascertain what our duty is, in any emergency, we must apply well-settled and generally accepted principles. It is our duty to avoid stealing, no matter whether the thing to be stolen is of great or little value. It is our duty to avoid killing a human being, no matter where the human being lives or to what race or class he belongs.

Every one recognizes the obligation imposed upon individuals to observe both the human and the moral law, but . . . some deny the application of those laws to nations. . . .

Many may dare to do in crowds what they would not dare to do as individuals, but the moral character of an act is not determined by the number of those who join it. Force can defend a right, but force has never yet created a right. If it was true, as declared in the resolutions of intervention, that the Cubans "are and of right ought to be free and independent" (language taken from the Declaration of Independence), it is equally true that the Filipinos "are and of right ought to be free and independent."

The right of the Cubans to freedom was not based upon their proximity to the United States, nor upon the language which they spoke, nor yet upon the race or races to which they belonged. Congress by a practically unanimous vote declared that the principles enunciated at Philadelphia in 1776 were still alive and applicable to the Cubans. Who will draw a line between the natural rights of the Cubans and the Filipinos? Who will say that the former has a right to liberty and that the latter has no rights which we are bound to respect? And, if the Filipinos "are and of right ought to be free and independent," what right have we to force our government upon them without their consent? Before our duty can be ascertained their rights must be determined, and when their rights are once determined it is as much our duty to respect those rights as it was the duty of Spain to respect the rights of the people of Cuba or the duty of England to respect the rights of the American colonists. Rights never conflict; duties never clash. . . .

It is said that we have assumed before the world obligations which make it necessary for us to permanently maintain a government in the Philippine Islands. I reply . . . that the highest obligation of this nation is to be true to itself. No obligation to any particular nations, or to all the nations combined, can require the abandonment of our theory of government, and the substitution of doctrines against which our whole national life has been a protest. . . .

It is argued by some that the Filipinos are incapable of self-government and that, therefore, we owe it to the world to take control of them. . . . Henry Clay, in defending the right of the people of South America to self-government, said: "It is the doctrine of thrones that man is too ignorant to govern himself. . . ."

Clay was right. There are degrees of proficiency in the art of self-government, but it is a reflection upon the Creator to say that he denied to any people the capacity for self-government. Once admit that some people are capable of self-government and that others are not and that the capable people have a right to seize upon and govern the incapable, and you make force—brute force—the only foundation of government and invite the reign of a despot. I am not willing to believe that an all-wise and an all-loving God created the Filipinos and then left them thousands of years helpless until the islands attracted the attention of European nations. . . .

"Can we not govern colonies?" we are asked. The question is not what we can do, but what we ought to do. This nation can do whatever it desires to do, but it must accept responsibility for what it does. If the Constitution stands in the way, the people can amend the Constitution. I repeat, the nation can do whatever it desires to do, but it cannot avoid the natural and legitimate results of its own conduct.

The young man upon reaching his majority can do what he pleases. He can disregard the teachings of his parents; he can trample upon all that he has been taught to consider sacred; he can disobey the laws of the State, the laws of society and the laws of God. He can stamp failure upon his life, and make his very existence a curse to his fellow men, and he can bring his father and mother in sorrow to the grave; but he cannot annul the sentence, "The wages of sin is death."

And so with the nation. It is of age and it can do what it pleases; it can spurn the traditions of the past; it can repudiate the principles upon which the nation rests; it can employ force instead of reason; it can substitute might for right; it can conquer weaker people; it can exploit their lands, appropriate their property and kill their people, but it cannot repeal the moral law or escape the punishment decreed for the violation of human rights. . . .

The principal arguments . . . advanced by those who enter upon a defense of imperialism are:

First—That we must improve the present opportunity to become a world power and enter into international politics.

Second—That our commercial interests in the Philippine Islands and in the Orient make it necessary for us to hold the islands permanently.

Third—That the spread of the Christian religion will be facilitated by a colonial policy.

Fourth—That there is no honorable retreat from the position which the nation has taken.

The first argument is addrest to the nation's pride and the second to the nation's pocket-book. The third is intended for the church member and the fourth for the partizan.

It is sufficient answer to the first argument to say that for more than a century this nation has been a world power. For ten decades it has been the most potent influence in the world. Not only has it been a world power, but it has done more to shape the politics of the human race than all the other nations of the world combined. Because our Declaration of Independence was promulgated others have been promulgated. Because the patriots of 1776 fought for liberty others have fought for it. Because our Constitution was adopted other constitutions have been adopted.

The growth of the principle of self-government, planted on American soil, has been the overshadowing political fact of the nineteenth century. It has made this nation conspicuous among the nations and given it a place in history such as no other nation has ever enjoyed. Nothing has been able to check the onward march of this idea. I am not willing that this nation shall cast aside the omnipotent weapon of truth to seize again the weapons of physical warfare. I would not exchange the glory of this Republic for the glory of all the empires that have risen and fallen since time began.

The permanent chairman of the last Republican National Convention presented the pecuniary argument in all its baldness when he said:

We make no hypocritical pretense of being interested in the Philippines solely on account of others. While we regard the welfare of those people as a sacred trust, we regard the welfare of the American people first. We see our duty to ourselves as well as to others. We believe in trade expansion. By every legitimate means within the province of government and constitution we mean to stimulate the expansion of our trade and open new markets.

This is the commercial argument. It is based upon the theory that war can be rightly waged for pecuniary advantage, and that it is profitable to purchase trade by force and violence. . . .

The Democratic party is in favor of the expansion of trade. It would extend our trade by every legitimate and peaceful means; but it is not willing to make merchandise of human blood.

But a war of conquest is as unwise as it is unrighteous. A harbor and coaling station in the Philippines would answer every trade and military necessity and such a concession could have been secured at any time without difficulty.

It is not necessary to own people in order to trade with them. We carry on trade today with every part of the world, and our commerce has expanded more rapidly than the commerce of any European empire. We do not own Japan or China, but we trade with their people. We have not absorbed the republics of Central and South America, but we trade with them. It has not been necessary to have any political connection with Canada or the nations of Europe in order to trade with them. Trade cannot be permanently profitable unless it is voluntary.

When trade is secured by force, the cost of securing it and retaining it must be taken out of the profits, and the profits are never large enough to cover the expense. Such a system would never be defended but for the fact that the expense is borne by all the people, while the profits are enjoyed by a few. . . .

The pecuniary argument, though more effective with certain classes, is not likely to be used so often or presented with so much enthusiasm as the religious argument. . . .

The religious argument varies in positiveness from a passive belief that Providence delivered the Filipinos into our hands, for their good and our glory, to the exultation of the minister who said that we ought to "thrash the natives (Filipinos) until they understand who we are," and that "every bullet sent, every cannon shot and every flag waved means righteousness."

We cannot approve of this doctrine in one place unless we are willing to apply it everywhere. If there is poison in the blood of the hand it will ultimately reach the heart. It is equally true that forcible Christianity, if planted under the American flag in the far-away Orient, will sooner or later be transplanted upon American soil.

If true Christianity consists in carrying out in our daily lives the teachings of Christ, who will say that we are commanded to civilize with dynamite and proselyte with the sword? He who would declare the divine will must prove his authority either by Holy Writ or by evidence of a special dispensation.

Imperialism finds no warrant in the Bible. Love, not force, was the weapon of the Nazarene; sacrifice for others, not the exploitation of them, was His method of reaching the human heart. A missionary recently told me that the Stars and Stripes once saved his life because his assailant recognized our flag as a flag that had no blood upon it.

Let it be known that our missionaries are seeking souls instead of sovereignty; let it be known that instead of being the advance guard of conquering armies, they are going forth to help and uplift, having their loins girt about with truth and their feet shod with the preparation of the gospel of peace, wearing the breastplate of righteousness and carrying the sword of the spirit; let it be known that they are citizens of a nation which respects the rights of the citizens of other nations as carefully as it protects the rights of its own citizens, and the welcome given to our missionaries will be more cordial than the welcome extended to the missionaries of any other nation.

The argument made by some that it was unfortunate for the nation that it had anything to do with the Philippine Islands, but that the naval victory at Manila made the permanent acquisition of those islands necessary, is also unsound. We won a naval victory at Santiago, but that did not compel us to hold Cuba.

The shedding of American blood in the Philippine Islands does not make it imperative that we should retain possession forever; American blood was shed at San Juan Hill and El Caney, and yet the President has promised the Cubans independence. The fact that the American flag floats over Manila does not compel us to exercise perpetual sovereignty over the islands; the American flag waves over Havana to-day, but the President has promised to haul it down when the flag of the Cuban Republic is ready to rise in its place. Better a thousand times that our flag in the Orient give way to a flag representing the idea of self-government than that the flag of this Republic should become the flag of an empire. . . .

When our opponents are unable to defend their position by argument they fall back upon the assertion that it is destiny, and insist that we must submit to it, no matter how much it violates our moral precepts and our principles of government. This is a complacent philosophy. It obliterates the distinction between right and wrong and makes individuals and nations the helpless victims of circumstance.

Destiny is the subterfuge of the invertebrate, who, lacking the courage to oppose error, seeks some plausible excuse for supporting it. Washington said that the destiny of the republican form of government was deeply, if not finally, staked on the experiment entrusted to the American people. How different Washington's definition of destiny from the Republican definition!

The Republicans say that this nation is in the hands of destiny; Washington believed that not only the destiny of our own nation but the destiny of the republican form of government throughout the world was entrusted to American hands. Immeasurable responsibility! The destiny of this republic is in the hands of its own people, and upon the success of the experiment here rests the hope of humanity. No exterior force can disturb this republic, and no foreign influence should be permitted to change its course. What the future has in store for this nation no one has authority to declare, but each individual has his own idea of the nation's mission, and he owes it to his country as well as to himself to contribute as best he may to the fulfilment of that mission. . . .

I can conceive of a national destiny surpassing the glories of the present and the past—a destiny which meets the responsibilities of to-day and measures up to the possibilities of the future. Behold a republic, resting securely upon the foundation stones quarried by revolutionary patriots from the mountain of eternal truth—a republic applying in practise and proclaiming to the world the self-evident propositions that all men are created equal; that they are endowed by their Creator with inalienable rights; that governments are instituted among men to secure these rights, and that governments derive their just powers from the consent of the governed. Behold a republic in which civil and religious liberty stimulate all to earnest endeavor and in which the law restrains every hand uplifted for a neighbor's injury—a republic in which every citizen is a sovereign, but in which no one cares or dares to wear a crown. Behold a republic standing erect while empires all around are bowed beneath the weight of their own armaments—a republic whose flag is loved while other flags are only feared. Behold a republic increasing in population, in wealth, in strength and in influence, solving the problems of civilization and hastening the coming of an universal brotherhood—a republic which shakes thrones and dissolves aristocracies by its silent example and gives light and inspiration to those who sit in darkness. Behold a republic gradually but surely becoming the supreme moral factor in the world's progress and the accepted arbiter of the world's disputes—a republic whose history, like the path of the just, "is as the shining light that shineth more and more unto the perfect day."

THE OPEN DOOR

. . . The policy of the government of the United States is to seek a solution which may bring about permanent safety and peace to China . . . and safeguard for the world the principle of equal and impartial trade with all parts of the Chinese Empire.

—JOHN HAY, 1899.

*E*ARNESTLY DESIROUS to remove any cause of irritation and to insure at the same time to the commerce of all nations in China the undoubted benefits which should accrue from a formal recognition by the various powers claiming "spheres of interest" that they shall enjoy perfect equality of treatment for their commerce and navigation within such "spheres," the Government of the United States would be pleased to see His German Majesty's Government give formal assurances and lend its cooperation in securing like assurances from the other interested powers that each within its respective sphere of whatever influence—

First. Will in no way interfere with any treaty port or any vested interest within any so-called "sphere of interest" or leased territory it may have in China.

Second. That the Chinese treaty tariff of the time being shall apply to all merchandise landed or shipped to all such ports as are within said "sphere of interest" (unless they be "free ports"), no matter to

Secretary of State John Hay to the United States Ambassador in Germany, September 6, 1899; to all United States Embassies, July 3, 1900. U.S. Department of State, *Foreign Relations of the United States*, 1899; 1901, Appendix, p. 12.

what nationality it may belong, and that duties so leviable shall be collected by the Chinese Government.

Third. That it will levy no higher harbor dues on vessels of another nationality frequenting any port in such "sphere" then shall be levied on vessels of its own nationality, and no higher railroad charges over lines built, controlled, or operated within its "sphere" on merchandise belonging to citizens or subjects of other nationalities transported through such "sphere" than shall be levied on similar merchandise belonging to its own nationals transported over equal distances.

In this critical posture of affairs in China it is deemed appropriate to define the attitude of the United States as far as present circumstances permit this to be done. We adhere to the policy initiated by us in 1857, of peace with the Chinese nation, of furtherance of lawful commerce, and of protection of lives and property of our citizens by all means guaranteed under extraterritorial treaty rights and by the law of nations. If wrong be done to our citizens we propose to hold the responsible authors to the uttermost accountability. We regard the condition at Pekin as one of virtual anarchy, whereby power and responsibility are practically devolved upon the local provincial authorities. So long as they are not in overt collusion with rebellion and use their power to protect foreign life and property we regard them as representing the Chinese people, with whom we seek to remain in peace and friendship. The purpose of the President is, as it has been heretofore, to act concurrently with the other powers, first, in opening up communication with Pekin and rescuing the American officials, missionaries, and other Americans who are in danger; secondly, in affording all possible protection everywhere in China to American life and property; thirdly, in guarding and protecting all legitimate American interests; and fourthly, in aiding to prevent a spread of the disorders to the other provinces of the Empire and a recurrence of such disasters. It is, of course, too early to forecast the means of attaining this last result; but the policy of the government of the United States is to seek a solution which may bring about permanent safety and peace to China, preserve Chinese territorial and administrative entity, protect all rights guaranteed to friendly powers by treaty and international law, and safeguard for the world the principle of equal and impartial trade with all parts of the Chinese Empire.

VII. Missionary State: First Phase

The assassination of McKinley in 1901 made Theodore Roosevelt president, and in office he remained an activist. But when World War I arrived, bringing with it the first great test of how the New World would behave in relation to the Old, the president was Woodrow Wilson, a Democrat and the inheritor of the party that Bryan had dominated.

Wilson's outlook was neither Bryan's nor Roosevelt's. Like Bryan, he held that America's example should shine for all men and that the United States should not extend its dominion or rule. Like Roosevelt, however, he was willing to apply the nation's power in order to achieve Americanization abroad. In the beginning of his administration, he attempted to impose democracy on Mexico, and, after the European war began, he demanded that Germany fight according to international law. When she did not, he led his nation into war against her. At the peace conference in 1919 he then endeavored to write a treaty for Europe that would embody American principles—self-government for subject peoples, democracy, written law prescribing rules for nations as well as individuals, minimal armaments, and submission of all international issues to processes of debate.

While these were principles that most Americans endorsed, some felt that Wilson's treaty made too many compromises with them;

others feared that signing it might entail using force to back it up. The man who gave voice to these criticisms, as to some of the widespread doubts about Wilson's policies as a neutral, was Senator Henry Cabot Lodge of Massachusetts, a follower of Roosevelt's but also (though he would have been the first to deny it) of Bryan's.

WOODROW WILSON AND

HENRY CABOT LODGE ON

AMERICAN AIMS

In emphasizing the points which must unite us in sympathy and in spiritual interest with the Latin American peoples we are only emphasizing the points of our own life, and we should prove ourselves untrue to our own traditions if we proved ourselves untrue friends to them. —WOODROW WILSON, 1913.

*T*HE FUTURE ... is going to be very different for this hemisphere from the past. These States lying to the south of us, which have always been our neighbors, will now be drawn closer to us by innumerable ties, and, I hope, chief of all, by the tie of a common understanding of each other. Interest does not tie nations together; it sometimes separates them. But sympathy and understanding does unite them, and I believe that by the new route that is just about to be opened [the Panama canal], while we physically cut two continents asunder, we spiritually unite them. It is a spiritual union which we seek.

I wonder if you realize, I wonder if your imaginations have been filled with the significance of the tides of commerce. . . . Columbus

Speech before the Southern Commercial Congress, Mobile, Alabama, October 27, 1913. Albert Shaw, Ed., *The Messages and Papers of Woodrow Wilson.* Review of Reviews Corporation, New York, 1924, vol. I, pp. 32-36.

set out not to discover America, for he did not know that it existed, but to discover the eastern shores of Asia. He set sail for Cathay and stumbled upon America. With that change in the outlook of the world, what happened? England, that had been at the back of Europe with an unknown sea behind her, found that all things had turned as if upon a pivot and she was at the front of Europe; and since then all the tides of energy and enterprise that have issued out of Europe have seemed to be turned westward across the Atlantic. But you will notice that they have turned westward chiefly north of the Equator and that it is the northern half of the globe that has seemed to be filled with the media of intercourse and of sympathy and of common understanding.

Do you not see now what is about to happen? These great tides which have been running along parallels of latitude will now swing southward athwart parallels of latitude, and that opening gate at the Isthmus of Panama will open the world to a commerce that she has not known before, a commerce of intelligence, of thought and sympathy between North and South. The Latin American States, which, to their disadvantage, have been off the main lines, will now be on the main lines. . . . [W]e are closing one chapter in the history of the world and are opening another, of great, unimaginable significance.

There is one peculiarity about the history of the Latin American States which I am sure they are keenly aware of. You hear of "concessions" to foreign capitalists in Latin America. You do not hear of concessions to foreign capitalists in the United States. They are not granted concessions. They are invited to make investments. The work is ours, though they are welcome to invest in it. We do not ask them to supply the capital and do the work. It is an invitation, not a privilege; and States that are obliged, because their territory does not lie within the main field of modern enterprise and action, to grant concessions are in this condition, that foreign interests are apt to dominate their domestic affairs, a condition of affairs always dangerous and apt to become intolerable. What these States are going to see, therefore, is an emancipation from the subordination, which has been inevitable, to foreign enterprise and an assertion of the splendid character, which, in spite of these difficulties, they have again and again been able to demonstrate. . . .

We must prove ourselves their friends, and champions upon terms of equality and honor. You cannot be friends upon any other terms than upon the terms of equality. You cannot be friends at all except upon the terms of honor. We must show ourselves friends by comprehending their interest whether it squares with our own interest or not. It is a very perilous thing to determine the foreign policy of a nation in the terms of material interest. It not only is unfair to those with whom you are dealing, but it is degrading as regards your own actions.

Comprehension must be the soil in which shall grow all the fruits of friendship, and there is a reason and a compulsion lying behind all this which is dearer than anything else to the thoughtful men of America. I mean the development of constitutional liberty in the world. Human rights, national integrity, and opportunity as against material interests—that, ladies and gentlemen, is the issue which we now have to face. I want to take this occasion to say that the United States will never again seek one additional foot of territory by conquest. She will devote herself to showing that she knows how to make honorable and fruitful use of the territory she has, and she must regard it as one of the duties of friendship to see that from no quarter are material interests made superior to human liberty and national opportunity. I say this, not with a single thought that anyone will gainsay it, but merely to fix in our consciousness what our real relationship with the rest of America is. It is the relationship of a family of mankind devoted to the development of true constitutional liberty. We know that that is the soil out of which the best enterprise springs. We know that this is a cause which we are making in common with our neighbors, because we have had to make it for ourselves. . . .

I know what the response of the thought and heart of America will be to the program I have outlined, because America was created to realize a program like that. This is not America because it is rich. This is America because it has set up for a great population great opportunities of material prosperity. America is a name which sounds in the ears of men everywhere as a synonym with individual opportunity because a synonym of individual liberty. I would rather belong to a poor nation that was free than to a rich nation that had ceased to be in love with liberty. But we shall not be poor if we love liberty, because the nation that loves liberty truly sets every man free to do his best and be his best, and that means the release of all the splendid energies of a great people who think for themselves. . . .

In emphasizing the points which must unite us in sympathy and in spiritual interest with the Latin American peoples we are only emphasizing the points of our own life, and we should prove ourselves untrue to our own traditions if we proved ourselves untrue friends to them. . . .

No peace can last, or ought to last, which does not recognize and accept the principle that governments derive all their just powers from the consent of the governed, and that no right anywhere exists to hand peoples about from sovereignty to sovereignty as if they were property. —WOODROW WILSON, 1917.

*I*N EVERY DISCUSSION of the peace that must end this war it is taken for granted that that peace must be followed by some definite concert of power which will make it virtually impossible that any such catastrophe should ever overwhelm us again. Every lover of mankind, every sane and thoughtful man must take that for granted. . . .

Peace Without Victory, Address to Congress, January 22, 1917. *Ibid.*, pp. 349-356.

It is inconceivable that the people of the United States should play no part in that great enterprise. To take part in such a service will be the opportunity for which they have sought to prepare themselves by the very principles and purposes of their policy and the approved practices of their Government ever since the days when they set up a new nation in the high and honorable hope that it might in all that it was and did show mankind the way to liberty. They cannot in honor withhold the service to which they are now about to be challenged. They do not wish to withhold it. But they owe it to themselves and to the other nations of the world to state the conditions under which they will feel free to render it.

That service is nothing less than this, to add their authority and their power to the authority and force of other nations to guarantee peace and justice throughout the world. Such a settlement cannot now be long postponed. It is right that before it comes this Government should frankly formulate the conditions upon which it would feel justified in asking our people to approve its formal and solemn adherence to a League for Peace. I am here to attempt to state those conditions.

The present war must first be ended; but we owe it to candor and to a just regard for the opinion of mankind to say that, so far as our participation in guarantees of future peace is concerned, it makes a great deal of difference in what way and upon what terms it is ended. The treaties and agreements which bring it to an end must embody terms which will create a peace that is worth guaranteeing and preserving, a peace that will win the approval of mankind, not merely a peace that will serve the several interests and immediate aims of the nations engaged. . . .

No covenant of cooperative peace that does not include the peoples of the New World can suffice to keep the future safe against war; and yet there is only one sort of peace that the peoples of America could join in guaranteeing. The elements of that peace must be elements that engage the confidence and satisfy the principles of the American governments, elements consistent with their political faith and with the practical convictions which the peoples of America have once for all embraced and undertaken to defend.

I do not mean to say that any American government would throw any obstacle in the way of any terms of peace the governments now at war might agree upon, or seek to upset them when made, whatever they might be. I only take it for granted that mere terms of peace between the belligerents will not satisfy even the belligerents themselves. Mere agreements may not make peace secure. It will be absolutely necessary that a force be created as a guarantor of the permanency of the settlement so much greater than the force of any nation now engaged or any alliance hitherto formed or projected that no nation, no probable combination of nations could face or withstand it. If the peace presently to be made is to endure, it must be a peace made secure by the organized major force of mankind.

The terms of the immediate peace agreed upon will determine whether it is a peace for which such a guarantee can be secured. The question upon which the whole future peace and policy of the world depends is this: Is the present war a struggle for a just and secure peace, or only for a new balance of power? If it be only a struggle for a new balance of power, who will guarantee, who can guarantee, the stable equilibrium of the new arrangement? Only a tranquil Europe can be a stable Europe. There must be, not a balance of power, but a community of power; not organized rivalries, but an organized common peace. . . .

First of all, . . . it must be a peace without victory. . . . Victory would mean peace forced upon the loser, a victor's terms imposed upon the vanquished. It would be accepted in humiliation, under duress, at an intolerable sacrifice, and would leave a sting, a resentment, a bitter memory upon which terms of peace would rest, not permanently, but only as upon quicksand. Only a peace between equals can last. Only a peace the very principle of which is equality and a common participation in a common benefit. The right state of mind, the right feeling between nations, is as necessary for a lasting peace as is the just settlement of vexed questions of territory or of racial and national allegiance.

The equality of nations upon which peace must be founded if it is to last must be an equality of rights; the guarantees exchanged must neither recognize nor imply a difference between big nations and small, between those that are powerful and those that are weak. Right must be based upon the common strength, not upon the individual strength, of the nations upon whose concert peace will depend. Equality of territory or of resources there of course cannot be; nor any other sort of equality not gained in the ordinary peaceful and legitimate development of the peoples themselves. But no one asks or expects anything more than an equality of rights. Mankind is looking now for freedom of life, not for equipoises of power.

And there is a deeper thing involved than even equality of right among organized nations. No peace can last, or ought to last, which does not recognize and accept the principle that governments derive all their just powers from the consent of the governed, and that no right anywhere exists to hand peoples about from sovereignty to sovereignty as if they were property. . . .

I speak of this, not because of any desire to exalt an abstract political principle which has always been held very dear by those who have sought to build up liberty in America, but for the same reason that I have spoken of the other conditions of peace which seem to me clearly indispensable—because I wish frankly to uncover realities. Any peace which does not recognize and accept this principle will inevitably be upset. It will not rest upon the affections or the convictions of mankind. The ferment of spirit of whole populations will fight subtly and constantly against it, and all the world will sympathize. The world can be at peace only if its life is stable, and there can be no stability where the will is in rebellion, where there is not tranquility of spirit and a sense of justice, of freedom, and of right. . . .

I have spoken upon these great matters without reserve and with the utmost explicitness because it has seemed to me to be necessary if the world's yearning desire for peace was anywhere to find free voice and utterance. . . . I feel confident that I have said what the people of the United States would wish me to say. May I not add that I hope and believe that I am in effect speaking for liberals and friends of humanity in every nation and of every programme of liberty. I would fain believe that I am speaking for the silent mass of mankind everywhere who have as yet had no place or opportunity to speak their real hearts out concerning the death and ruin they see to have come already upon the persons and the home they hold most dear.

And in holding out the expectation that the people and Government of the United States will join the other civilized nations of the world in guaranteeing the permanence of peace upon such terms as I have named I speak with the greater boldness and confidence because it is clear to every man who can think that there is in this promise no breach in either our traditions or our policy as a nation, but a fulfilment, rather, of all that we have professed or striven for.

I am proposing, as it were, that the nations should with one accord adopt the doctrine of President Monroe as the doctrine of the world: that no nation should seek to extend its polity over any other nation or people, but that every people should be left free to determine its own polity, its own way of development, unhindered, unthreatened, unafraid, the little along with the great and powerful.

I am proposing that all nations henceforth avoid entangling alliances which would draw them into competitions of power; catch them in a net of intrigue and selfish rivalry, and disturb their own affairs with influences intruded from without. There is no entangling alliance in a concert of power. When all unite to act in the same sense and with the same purpose all act in the common interest and are free to live their own lives under a common protection.

I am proposing government by the consent of the governed. . . .

These are American principles, American policies. We could stand for no others. And they are also the principles and policies of forward looking men and women everywhere, of every modern nation, of every enlightened community. They are the principles of mankind and must prevail.

As a preliminary of the peace which we are to help enforce must we insist that it cannot exist if there are any people under any Government who have been handed from sovereignty to sovereignty as if they were property? I am not contesting the justice of the principle —far from it—but we may well ask how we are going to compel the adoption of that principle by other Governments. . . .

—HENRY CABOT LODGE, 1917.

*I*T IS NOT NECESSARY, of course, to say anything as to the many general and just observations made by the President in regard to the horrors and miseries of war, or the dangers and complications with which the present conflict threatens the United States, or as to his or our duty as servants of humanity. . . .

In all these declarations we must be cordially and thoroughly of one mind. All that I desire to do is to speak briefly of the substantive propositions contained in the President's address and, by analysis, discover, if I can, to precisely what policies and course of action he is undertaking to commit the country. . . .

The President says that a peace won by victory would leave a bitter memory upon which peace terms could not rest permanently but only as upon quicksand. There has been pretty constant fighting in this unhappy world ever since the time when history begins its

Lodge's reply to Wilson. Speech in the United States Senate, February 1, 1917. *Congressional Record*, 64th Congress, 2nd session, pp. 2364-2370.

records, and in speaking of lasting peace in terms of history we can only speak comparatively. . . . It is a little hasty . . . to say that no peace can endure which is the fruit of victory. The peace which lasts is the peace which rests on justice and righteousness, and if it is a just and righteous peace it makes no difference whether it is based on the compromises and concessions of treaties or upon victories in the field. . . .

The next condition precedent stated by the President without which we can have no peace that "can or ought to last" is the universal acceptance of the idea that governments derive all their just powers from the consent of the governed, and that any peace which does not recognize and accept this principle will inevitably be upset. Must the fact that any given government rests on the consent of the governed be determined by a popular vote or by the general acceptance by the people of the existing form of government? Who is to decide whether the principle is recognized under the different governments of the world with whom we are to form the League for Peace "supported by the organized major force of mankind" . . .? As a preliminary of the peace which we are to help enforce must we insist that it cannot exist if there are any people under any Government who have been handed from sovereignty to sovereignty as if they were property? I am not contesting the justice of the principle—far from it—but we may well ask how we are going to compel the adoption of that principle by other Governments, and this is no idle question but a real and practical one which cannot be evaded. . . .

The President says that he proposes, as it were, that the nations with one accord should adopt the doctrine of President Monroe as the doctrine of the world. In the effort which I am making to uncover the realities which lie behind the President's propositions and to avoid "the soft concealments" to which he justly objects, I do not find it easy to determine precisely what is meant by making the doctrine of President Monroe the doctrine of the world. . . . When we examine the message of 1823 it will be observed that the Monroe doctrine is strictly local in its application; that is, it applies only to the American hemisphere and is based on the theory that there are two spheres in the world which are entirely separate in their political interests. How are we to reframe the first portion of the Monroe doctrine so as to give it a world-wide application? It asserts that the American continents are not to be considered as subjects for future colonization by any European power. How is this proposition to be turned into a world doctrine? If all the European powers accepted that doctrine and agreed with us that they would attempt no colonization here we should have the recognition of the doctrine by European powers, but the doctrine would apply to the same territory as before. How are we to turn into a world doctrine President Monroe's second statement that he should regard it as an unfriendly act if any European power interfered with the independence of any American Government? Is the transformation to be effected by having Europe and Asia and Africa adopt a doctrine that there shall be no colonies established by any power on any of these great continents and that if, for example, any European power should establish a new colony somewhere in Africa we should regard it as an unfriendly act? It has been suggested that the Monroe doctrine would cover the protection of small nations. The Monroe doctrine has nothing to do with the rights of small or great powers as such. Its declared purpose was simply to protect the independence of all American States, great and small, from the interference of Europe and to prohibit European colonization. . . . The Monroe doctrine defined our position and defined nobody else's position, and if we are to extend that doctrine to the other nations the only sanction it could carry would be that we should regard European colonization in all continents as an unfriendly act. Or does the President's proposition mean that the Monroe doctrine is to be extended to all the world and thereby be abandoned . . .?

I have tried very briefly to set forth the conditions precedent which the President says are essential to a lasting peace. I have endeavored in a very general and imperfect way to "uncover the realities" and to get rid of all "soft concealments." Now, having clearly in our minds these conditions precedent, vital to the establishment of a last-

ing peace which we are to help bring about, I desire to consider
the part which we are to take in maintaining it. . . . If the peace of
the world is to be maintained as the peace of a city or the internal
peace of a nation is maintained, it must be maintained in the same
way—by force. . . .

Everyone must feel, as I do, the enormous importance of securing
in some way the peace of the world and relieving the future of humanity from such awful struggles as that which is now going on in
Europe, but if the only advance is to be made through the creation
of an international force we are brought face to face with the difficulties of that system. . . .

The first question that would occur to any one of us is what the
numbers of the league force will be. . . . Will it not be worth while
to pause a moment before we commit ourselves to an army of
500,000 men, to be held ready for war at the pleasure of other nations in whose councils we shall have but one vote if we are true to
the President's policy of the equality of nations . . .?

If we are to adhere to the principle of the equality of nations laid
down by the President, each nation, great and small, having equality
of rights, would have an equal voice in the decision of the league,
and a majority would set the forces of the league in motion. It might
happen that the majority would be composed of the smaller and
weaker nations, who, if they are to have equality of rights, would thus
be enabled to precipitate the greater nations into war, into a war perhaps with one of the greatest nations of the league. In the present
state of human nature and public opinion is it probable that any nation will bind itself to go to war at the command of other nations and
furnish its army and navy to be disposed of as the majority of other
nations may see fit? It seems to me that it is hardly possible, and yet
in what other way can we come to the practical side of this question?
In what other way are you to enforce the decisions of the league? If
you undertake to limit the . . . disputes between nations which the
league shall decide, you will not be able to go beyond the limits already imposed in voluntary arbitration, and there will be no need

of force. If a real advance is to be made, you must go beyond those
limitations, you must agree to submit to the decision of the league
questions which no nations will now admit to be arbitrable. You
would be compelled, if a decree of the league were resisted, to go to
war without any action on the part of Congress and wholly on the
command of other nations. We are all anxious to promote peace in
every possible way, but if we are to maintain the peace of the world
by force it can only be maintained in the way I have described, and no
amount of shouting about the blessings of peace will relieve us from
the obligations or the necessities imposed by putting force behind the
peace of the world as we put it behind the peace of a city.

Let us now consider this plan from our own point of view alone
and with reference solely to the United States. The policy of the
United States hitherto has been the policy laid down by Washington
and its corollary expressed in the message of President Monroe.
Washington declared that we had a set of interests separate from
those of Europe and that European political questions did not concern us. Monroe declared that we had a set of questions which did
not concern Europe, and that, as we did not meddle with Europe,
Europe must not meddle with us. . . . The wisdom of Washington's
policy, supplemented by that of Monroe, has been demonstrated by
the experience of more than a century. . . . We are now invited to
depart from it by giving our adherence to a league for peace when
the present war closes, without knowing how far it is proposed to go
or what is to be demanded of us. If an effective league for peace
among the nations is to be made it must be one backed by the force
which the President has described. Are we prepared to commit ourselves to a purely general proposition without knowing where we are
going or what is to be demanded of us, except that we shall be compelled to furnish our quota of military and naval forces to the service
of a league in which we shall have but one voice? We are asked to
place ourselves in a position where our military forces could be used
for war by the decree of other nations. This would be a very momentous step. Surely we ought to pause and consider very carefully and

know every detail before we commit ourselves to any vague, general propositions involving such serious results and responsibilities.

The first service which the United States can render to the cause of peace is to preserve its own. I do not mean within its own borders, but to preserve its peace with the other nations of the earth. This can be done in only one way—by the most absolute and scrupulous observance of every treaty or agreement that we enter into; by the termination of all treaties for arbitration which we know well we should not under certain conditions and in time of stress regard, for no such war-breeding treaties ought to cumber the ground; and, lastly, by the establishment of such national defenses, both by land and sea, as to insure our country, so far as it can be done, from wanton attack. . . . We have no means of repelling the invasion of a great power as it must be repelled, and such weakness, combined with great wealth, constitutes an invitation and a temptation to war. Against that danger we should ensure ourselves by adequate national defenses, and by reducing the danger of war being forced upon us we to that extent promote the peace of mankind and we likewise put ourselves in a position where our influence and power in the world for the maintenance of general peace would be enormously increased. The next thing to which we ought to address ourselves on the conclusion of this war should be the rehabilitation and reestablishment of international law. International law represents the great mass of customs and usages which have become law and which have been observed, cited, and referred to by the nations. International law has had an ever-increasing power in guiding and controlling the conduct of nations toward each other. The fact that it has been violated and disregarded in many instances during the present conflict is no reason for adopting the counsel of despair and saying that it is of no value and must be abandoned. It is of enormous value and should be restored and upbuilt . . . with all the energy and influence which we can bring to bear. We should try also, within the necessary and natural limits, to extend the use of voluntary arbitration, so far as possible, and create, as we can well do, a powerful public opinion behind the system and behind the maintenance of peace. We can also do much in urging a general reduction of armaments by all nations.

It may be said that these are but slight improvements and but moderate advances. This may all be true, but what I propose has at least this merit—it is not visionary, and I suggest nothing which is not practical and reasonable and which will not, within its limitations, do substantial good. If there is any way in which we can go further without creating a worse condition nobody will be more rejoiced than I; but I do not wish to plunge blindly forward, misled by phrases and generalities, into undertakings which threaten worse results than the imperfect conditions now existing. We are as a people altogether too prone to be satisfied with words; to believe that we advance the cause of peace or any good cause merely by shouting for it. When we approach such questions as are involved in our relations with the other nations of the earth and such a mighty issue as the maintenance of the world's peace, to be misled by words and to take words for deeds would be a fatal error. Whatever we decide to do, let us know precisely what we are doing and what we may reasonably expect. . . .

This war will end; the passions of mankind will die down; individual ambitions will vanish with the evanescent beings who cherish them; but the Republic and the American people will remain. Let us beware how we take any steps which may precipitate this country and the people who are to come after us and whose inheritance it is, into dangers which no man can foresee. We cannot secure our own safety or build up the lasting peace of the world upon peace at any price. The peace of the world, to be enduring, must be based on righteousness at any cost.

WOODROW WILSON AND

HENRY CABOT LODGE ON

THE DISPUTE OVER

THE LEAGUE OF NATIONS

Our isolation was ended twenty years ago. . . . There can be no question of our ceasing to be a world power. The only question is whether we can refuse the moral leadership that is offered us, whether we shall accept or reject the confidence of the world.
                                        —WOODROW WILSON, 1919.

T HE TREATY OF PEACE with Germany was signed at Versailles on the twenty-eighth of June. I avail myself of the earliest opportunity to lay the treaty before you for ratification and to inform you with regard to the work of the Conference by which that treaty was formulated. . . .

It would be presuming in me to attempt to explain the questions which arose or the many diverse elements that entered into them. I shall attempt something less ambitious than that and more clearly suggested by my duty to report to the Congress the part it seemed necessary for my colleagues and me to play as the representatives of the Government of the United States.

Address to the Senate, presenting the Peace Treaty, July 10, 1919. Shaw, *op. cit.*, vol. II, pp. 698-712.

That part was dictated by the role America had played in the war and by the expectations that had been created in the minds of the peoples with whom we had associated ourselves in that great struggle.

The United States entered the war upon a different footing from every other nation except our associates on this side of the sea. We entered it, not because our material interests were directly threatened or because any special treaty obligations to which we were parties had been violated, but only because we saw the supremacy, and even the validity, of right everywhere put in jeopardy and free government likely to be everywhere imperiled by the intolerable aggression of a power which respected neither right nor obligation and whose very system of government flouted the rights of the citizen as against the autocratic authority of his governors. And in the settlements of the peace we have sought no special reparation for ourselves, but only the restoration of right and the assurance of liberty everywhere that the effects of the settlement were to be felt. We entered the war as the disinterested champions of right and we interested ourselves in the terms of the peace in no other capacity.

The hopes of the nations allied against the Central Powers were at a very low ebb when our soldiers began to pour across the sea. There was everywhere amongst them, except in their stoutest spirits, a sombre foreboding of disaster. . . . The mere sight of our men,— of their vigor, of the confidence that showed itself in every movement of their stalwart figures and every turn of their swinging march, in their steady comprehending eyes and easy discipline, in the indomitable air that added spirit to everything they did,—made everyone who saw them that memorable day realize that something had happened that was much more than a mere incident in the fighting, something very different from the mere arrival of fresh troops. A great moral force had flung itself into the struggle. The fine physical force of those spirited men spoke of something more than bodily vigor. They carried the great ideals of a free people at their hearts and with that vision were unconquerable. Their very presence brought reassurance; their fighting made victory certain. . . .

They were for all the visible embodiment of America. What they did made America and all that she stood for a living reality in the thoughts not only of the people of France but also of tens of millions of men and women throughout all the toiling nations of a world standing everywhere in peril of its freedom and of the loss of everything it held dear, in deadly fear that its bonds were never to be loosed, its hopes forever to be mocked and disappointed.

And the compulsion of what they stood for was upon us who represented America at the peace table. It was our duty to see to it that every decision we took part in contributed, so far as we were able to influence it, to quiet the fears and realize the hopes of the peoples who had been living in that shadow, the nations that had come by our assistance to their freedom. It was our duty to do everything that it was within our power to do to make the triumph of freedom and of right a lasting triumph in the assurance of which men might everywhere live without fear. . . .

The role which America was to play in the Conference seemed determined . . . by the universal expectations of the nations whose representatives, drawn from all quarters of the globe, we were to deal with. . . . We had formulated the principles upon which the settlement was to be made,—the principles upon which the Armistice had been agreed to and the parleys of peace undertaken,—and no one doubted that our desire was to see the treaty of peace formulated along the actual lines of those principles,—and desired nothing else. We were welcomed as disinterested friends. We were resorted to as arbiters in many a difficult matter. It was recognized that our material aid would be indispensable in the days to come, when industry and credit would have to be brought back to their normal operation again and communities beaten to the ground assisted to their feet once more, and it was taken for granted, I am proud to say, that we would play the helpful friend in these things as in all others without prejudice or favor. We were generously accepted as the unaffected champions of what was right. It was a very responsible role to play; but I am happy to report that the fine group of Americans who helped with their expert advice in each part of the varied settlements sought in every transaction to justify the high confidence reposed in them.

And that confidence, it seems to me, is the measure of our opportunity and of our duty in the days to come, in which the new hope of the peoples of the world is to be fulfilled or disappointed. The fact that America is the friend of the nations, whether they be rivals or associates, is no new fact; it is only the discovery of it by the rest of the world that is new.

America may be said to have just reached her majority as a world power. It was almost exactly twenty-one years ago that the results of the war with Spain put us unexpectedly in possession of rich islands on the other side of the world and brought us into association with other governments in the control of the West Indies. It was regarded as a sinister and ominous thing by the statesmen of more than one European chancellory that we should have extended our power beyond the confines of our continental dominions. They were accustomed to think of new neighbors as a new menace, of rivals as watchful enemies. There were persons amongst us at home who looked with deep disapproval and avowed anxiety on such extensions of our national authority over distant islands and over peoples whom they feared we might exploit, not serve and assist. But we have not exploited them. We have been their friends and have sought to serve them. And our dominion has been a menace to no other nation. We redeemed our honor to the utmost in our dealings with Cuba. She is weak but absolutely free; and it is her trust in us that makes her free. Weak peoples everywhere stand ready to give us any authority among them that will assure them a like friendly oversight and direction. They know that there is no ground for fear in receiving us as their mentors and guides. Our isolation was ended twenty years ago; and now fear of us is ended also, our counsel and association sought after and desired. There can be no question of our ceasing to be a world power. The only question is whether we can refuse the moral leadership that is offered us, whether we shall accept or reject the confidence of the world.

The war and the Conference of Peace now sitting in Paris seem to me to have answered that question. Our participation in the war established our position among the nations and nothing but our own mistaken action can alter it. It was not an accident or a matter of sudden choice that we are no longer isolated and devoted to a policy which has only our own interest and advantage for its object. It was our duty to go in, if we were indeed the champions of liberty and of right. We answered to the call of duty in a way so spirited, so utterly without thought of what we spent of blood or treasure, so effective, so worthy of the admiration of true men everywhere, so wrought out of the stuff of all that was heroic, that the whole world saw at last, in the flesh, in noble action, a great deal asserted and vindicated, by a nation they had deemed material and now found to be compact of the spiritual forces that must free men of every nation from every unworthy bondage. It is thus that a new role and a new responsibility have come to this great nation that we honor and which we would all wish to lift to yet higher levels of service and achievement.

The stage is set, the destiny disclosed. It has come about by no plan of our conceiving, but by the hand of God who led us into this way. We cannot turn back. We can only go forward, with lifted eyes and freshened spirit, to follow the vision. It was of this that we dreamed at our birth. America shall in truth show the way. The light streams upon the path ahead, and nowhere else.

. . . There is a wide difference between taking a suitable part and bearing a due responsibility in world affairs and plunging the United States into every controversy and conflict on the face of the globe. By meddling in all the differences which may arise among any por-

*tion or fragment of humankind we simply fritter away our influence
and injure ourselves to no good purpose.*
                              —HENRY CABOT LODGE, 1919.

*T*HOSE OF US, Mr. President, who are either wholly opposed to
the league or who are trying to preserve the independence and the
safety of the United States by changing the terms of the league and
who are endeavoring to make the league, if we are to be a member of
it, less certain to promote war instead of peace, have been reproached
with selfishness in our outlook and with a desire to keep our country
in a state of isolation. So far as the question of isolation goes, it is impossible to isolate the United States. . . . I think no one now would
question that the Spanish War marked the entrance of the United
States into world affairs to a degree which had never obtained before.
It was both an inevitable and an irrevocable step, and our entrance
into the war with Germany certainly showed once and for all that the
United States was not unmindful of its world responsibilities. We
may set aside all this empty talk about isolation. Nobody expects to
isolate the United States or to make it a hermit Nation, which is a
sheer absurdity. But there is a wide difference between taking a suitable part and bearing a due responsibility in world affairs and plunging the United States into every controversy and conflict on the face
of the globe. By meddling in all the differences which may arise
among any portion or fragment of humankind we simply fritter away
our influence and injure ourselves to no good purpose. We shall be of
far more value to the world and its peace by occupying, so far as possible, the situation which we have occupied for the last 20 years and
by adhering to the policy of Washington and Hamilton, of Jefferson
and Monroe, under which we have risen to our present greatness
and prosperity. The fact that we have been separated by our geographical situation and by our consistent policy from the broils of

Lodge's summation in the U.S. Senate, August 12, 1919. *Congressional Record,* 65th
Congress, 1st session, pp. 404-410.

Europe has made us more than any one thing capable of performing the great work which we performed in the war against Germany, and our disinterestedness is of far more value to the world than our eternal meddling in every possible dispute could ever be.

Now, as to our selfishness. I have no desire to boast that we are better than our neighbors, but the fact remains that this Nation in making peace . . . had not a single selfish or individual interest to serve. All we asked was that Germany should be rendered incapable of again breaking forth, with all the horrors incident to German warfare, upon an unoffending world, and that demand was shared by every free nation and indeed by humanity itself. For ourselves we asked absolutely nothing. We have not asked any government or governments to guarantee our boundaries or our political independence. We have no fear in regard to either. We have sought no territory, no privileges, no advantages, for ourselves. That is the fact. It is apparent on the face of the treaty, I do not mean to reflect upon a single one of the powers with which we have been associated in the war against Germany, but there is not one of them which has not sought individual advantages for their own national benefit. . . . In the prosecution of the war we gave unstintedly American lives and American treasure. . . . We have not been ungenerous. We have been devoted to the cause of freedom, humanity, and civilization everywhere. Now we are asked, in the making of peace, to sacrifice our sovereignty in important respects, to involve ourselves almost without limit in the affairs of other nations, and to yield up policies and rights which we have maintained throughout our history. We are asked to incur liabilities to an unlimited extent and furnish assets at the same time which no man can measure. I think it is not only our right but our duty to determine how far we shall go. Not only must we look carefully to see where we are being led into endless disputes and entanglements, but we must not forget that we have in this country millions of people of foreign birth and parentage.

Our one great object is to make all these people Americans so that we may call on them to place America first and serve America as they have done in the war just closed. We cannot Americanize them if we are continually thrusting them back into the quarrels and difficulties of the countries from which they came to us. We shall fill this land with political disputes about the troubles and quarrels of other countries. We shall have a large portion of our people voting not on American questions and not on what concerns the United States but dividing on issues which concern foreign countries alone. This is an unwholesome and perilous condition to force upon this country. We must avoid it. We ought to reduce to the lowest possible point the foreign questions in which we involve ourselves. . . . It will all tend to delay the Americanization of our great population, and it is more important not only to the United States but to the peace of the world to make all these people good Americans than it is to determine that some piece of territory should belong to one European country rather than to another. For this reason I wish to limit strictly our interference in the affairs of Europe and of Africa. We have interests of our own in Asia and in the Pacific which we must guard upon our own account, but the less we undertake to play the part of umpire and thrust ourselves into European conflicts the better for the United States and for the world.

It has been reiterated here on this floor, and reiterated to the point of weariness, that in every treaty there is some sacrifice of sovereignty. That is not a universal truth by any means, but it is true of some treaties and it is a platitude which does not require reiteration. The question and the only question before us here is how much of our sovereignty we are justified in sacrificing. . . . Let us beware how we palter with our independence. We have not reached the great position from which we were able to come down into the field of battle and help save the world from tyranny by being guided by others. Our vast power has all been built up and gathered together by ourselves alone. We forced our way upward from the days of the Revolution, through a world often hostile and always indifferent. We owe no debt to anyone except to France in that Revolution, and those policies and those rights on which our power has been founded should never be lessened or weakened. It will be no service to the world to do so and it will be of intolerable injury to the United States. We will do our share. We are ready and anxious to help in all ways to preserve the world's peace. But we can do it best by not crippling ourselves.

I am as anxious as any human being can be to have the United States render every possible service to the civilization and the peace of mankind, but I am certain we can do it best by not putting ourselves in leading strings or subjecting our policies and our sovereignty to other nations. The independence of the United States is not only more precious to ourselves but to the world than any single possession. Look at the United States to-day. We have made mistakes in the past. We have had shortcomings. We shall make mistakes in the future and fall short of our own best hopes. But none the less is there any country to-day on the face of the earth which can compare with this in ordered liberty, in peace, and in the largest freedom . . . ? The United States is the world's best hope, but if you fetter her in the interests and quarrels of other nations, if you tangle her in the intrigues of Europe, you will destroy her power for good and endanger her very existence. Leave her to march freely through the centuries to come as in the years that have gone. Strong, generous, and confident, she has nobly served mankind. Beware how you trifle with your marvelous inheritance, this great land of ordered liberty, for if we stumble and fall, freedom and civilization everywhere will go down in ruin. . . .

Our first ideal is our country, and we see her in the future, as in the past, giving service to all her people and to the world. Our ideal of the future is that she should continue to render that service of her own free will. She has great problems of her own to solve, very grim and perilous problems, and a right solution, if we can attain to it, would largely benefit mankind. . . . Our ideal is to make her ever stronger and better and finer, because in that way alone, as we believe, can she be of the greatest service to the world's peace and to the welfare of mankind.

VIII. Missionary State: Second Phase

In the contest over ratification of the treaty of 1919 and participation in Wilson's League of Nations, Lodge was the victor. The United States withdrew into a self-imposed isolation, with successive presidents, Warren Harding, Calvin Coolidge, Herbert Hoover, and Franklin Delano Roosevelt (at least until 1937) taking the position that the nation should set an example for the world but take little active role in its affairs.

Then came the crises of 1938 and 1939, Munich, the annihilation of Czechoslovakia, Hitler's attack on Poland, and World War II. Roosevelt and a large part of the American public concluded that the foes of Hitler were fighting America's fight. Others disagreed. Remaining a vigorous commentator on current events, Hoover appealed to his countrymen not to identify with one side; participation in the war would not only spoil America's example but impair her physical as well as moral strength. Roosevelt, in his Four Freedoms address of January, 1941, heralding a program of massive lend-lease aid to nations fighting the Nazis, gave an eloquent reply, significant in that it emphasized practical as well as idealistic considerations.

When Germany's ally, Japan, attacked the American navy at Pearl Harbor, debate was silenced. Speaking for the whole people, or at

*least seeming to, Roosevelt could revive the idea of writing a peace
that would extend American ideals to the globe. And in the Charter
of the United Nations, which the Senate and public did not reject,
these ideals found expression.*

HERBERT HOOVER AND
FRANKLIN D. ROOSEVELT ON
THE ISSUES OF WORLD WAR II

If we join in this war the last great remaining strength will have been exhausted. And hope of world recuperation will have been delayed while Revolution marches unimpeded over the earth. . . . But if we remain out of war, we might, if we have the will to do so, use our unimpaired resources, our courage, our moral strength to do mankind infinite service. —HERBERT HOOVER, 1940.

THE FOUR HORSEMEN of the Apocalypse are on the march— War, Death, Famine, and Pestilence. Two thirds of the people in the world are at war. But coming before these old destroyers of mankind are five new Horsemen. The new cavalry are:

Imperialism, the destroyer of the independence of nations;

Intolerance, the destroyer of minorities;

State-ism, the destroyer of personal liberty;

Atheism, the destroyer of faith;

Hate, the destroyer of the unity of mankind.

These are the horsemen of the advance, preparing the way for War and Death. After War and Death sweep Famine and Pestilence.

From Herbert Hoover, "The Nine Horsemen and America," *Liberty Magazine*, June 5, 1940. *Further Addresses upon the American Road, 1938-1940.* Charles Scribner's Sons, New York, 1940, pp. 172-179.

And their camp-follower is Revolution.

Imperialism has already trampled down the independence of Ethiopia, Czechoslovakia, Poland, Albania, and Denmark. We have witnessed attacks upon China, Finland, and Norway, unable to defend themselves, and now the invasion of Holland and Belgium. And there seems to be more to come.

We have seen Intolerance destroy Jews, Christians, and racial minorities.

We have seen State-ism, expressed by the despotisms of Communism, Fascism, Nazi-ism, and Socialism, destroy liberty in Russia, in Germany, in Italy, and in a half dozen others. We have seen its infiltration through the world—including the United States.

Atheism has greatly shattered religious worship in Russia and Germany, and weakened beliefs in a score of others.

Hate has grown fiercely since before the first World War began, and its ravages are not alone between races but between classes and religious faiths.

And all the nine Horsemen have new weapons of destruction. Imperialism has become more dreadful by threat of destruction from the air. Propaganda, the weapon of Intolerance, of State-ism, of Atheism, of Hate, is more potent through our rapidity of communication. It now moves through the air over all borders and seas. It comes disguised in the home tongue. Hate has increased its voltage through cruelty of attack upon civilian men, women, and children by food blockade and death by the air. War is more destructive by our chemistry and our machines. Famine is made more terrible by the growth of great cities. Pestilence strikes right and left through the close net of our communications.

Only the Western Hemisphere is free of the full violence of these Horsemen. But they affect us. Our emotions are aroused. The attacks upon helpless small nations raise the indignation of all decent men and women. Our economic life is dislocated. The shadow of war hangs over all our decisions. And from our emotions there are Americans who sincerely believe that we ourselves should go to war. They feel we should be willing to sacrifice our youth and our future to restore liberty against aggression, to assure the recognition of law and human rights.

Reason calls for us not to send our sons into this war. Reason dictates that if we join the military operations of this war it means the abdication of the remaining seat of liberty in the world. Reason insists the Western Hemisphere should give sanctuary for peace in her flight from all the rest of the world. Reason is final in its demand that we prepare ourselves so that we may defend the Western Hemisphere.

To those who feel that we are not doing our part if we stay out I may suggest that we look ahead to the end of this war and examine a possibly greater service to mankind. This war will end some time either in victory or exhaustion. And in that relation we may well explore the grim work of the Horsemen Famine, Pestilence, and Hate.

FAMINE AND PESTILENCE

Western Europe for a hundred years, even in peacetime, has not produced sufficient food supplies for its own population. It has bought its food by the export of manufactured goods. But on top of this peacetime shortage of supplies, war at once diminishes the food production of every combatant nation. The imports of fodder are cut off or slackened, and the herds must be diminished. The drafting of manpower instantly diminishes the production of milk and of butter and of meat. The people eat into their animals, and when war ends their brood stock is depleted. Beyond this, planting of ground crops must be skimped. The harvesting is imperfect. And above all the nitrate fertilizers must be diverted to explosives.

It is true that each nation at modern war rations its population in hope of reducing its food consumption. Scarcity always raises prices and the food goes to those who have the most money. Rationing does secure more equality in distribution and control of prices. But it thrusts the hunger upon the civil population. Soldiers, munition-workers, and government officials are always well-fed. Thus hunger in the people falls hardest upon the women and children. But rationing has little effect upon the total consumption. War experience has proved that armies consume about twice as much food as the same men do when they are at peace. That is partly due to the greater physical need. It is partly due to the inevitable waste and destruction of food in camp, or by invasion and at sea.

Beyond all this the food production of the countries free of actual war is also demoralized, for the normal markets are interfered with by blockades and difficulties of credit to war purchasers. Prices are erratic and the farmer is uncertain. Some countries are wholly isolated. Thus production diminishes among neutrals, especially at the beginnings of wars.

By necessity of directing food supplies through the whole of the last war I watched these forces unfold with their millions of tragedies.

The food situation in the present war is already more desperate than at the same stage in the World War. Then, except for Belgium, there was no rationing of civil populations until the second or third year. In the present war every combatant country was on bread and meat cards within ninety days. In 1914 Russia was full of food; for years it has been in a state of semi-famine. Moreover today every neutral country in Europe out of fear has already mobilized almost its full manpower. The Balkan states, Holland, Belgium, Scandinavia and Italy will therefore also diminish in food production. The harvest of the Balkan States this year will now be reduced. Denmark, now unable to import fodder, must needs kill many of her animals. Many of these smaller nations are already on rations. And in invaded countries there is already famine. It sweeps over Poland.

Out of all these forces, *if this war is long continued,* there is but one implacable end. That end is the greatest famine in history. And from lowered vitality by famine comes Pestilence.

There was a great famine at the end of the World War. The dramatic events of peace-making obscured it. And as the people after the

Armistice were mostly fed by American action there was no major tragedy to attract headlines.

During the twenty-four months after the Armistice in 1918 we sent something over eighty billion pounds of concentrated foodstuffs from America to Europe. That was more food than we have exported to Europe in the whole of the last ten years combined. And this food went not only to our Allies but to our former enemies. And of pestilence, an army of typhus came down from Russia on a front a thousand miles long. At its height a million cases raged with a death-rate of a quarter of those stricken. Americans fought that battle and won.

Without all this service, famine, pestilence, and their end in Communism would have engulfed Europe. There would have been no peace of any sort.

After the Thirty Years' War a peace was made, and then it is said that one half of the population proceeded to die from famine and pestilence. There was no America then.

The conclusion of this observation is, "Who will stop the famine after the present war?"

THE SIXTH HORSEMAN——HATE

And now let us examine the destroyer Hate. He will have something to do with the American people. In his modern visage he is probably the greatest of all destroyers.

Racial hates developed to an intensity and over more people in the World War than ever before. From the miseries which followed it came another unparalleled development. That was class hate. Both of them have played a great part in this cataclysm of today.

Hate becomes completely inflamed in modern war. Nowadays fighting quickly flashes from wars between soldiers to wars against civilians. It was not so long ago that wars were fought entirely between soldiers. They had elements of chivalry and sportsmanship. When such wars were over hates did not long remain in courageous

men who fought against courageous men. But where war is made
against helpless civilians an implacable hate comes. Do we need to be
reminded of the seventy years of hate that survived in our country
from Sherman's March to the Sea?

As this war goes on the blockade of food supplies, the attacks on
civilians from the air, will take more toll from women and children.
As action between armies becomes more violent the long lists of dead
stream back from the front into the homes. From these wrongs and
sufferings imperishable hates will sink into every household.

And do not let us think that we had not in some lesser degree built
up hates in the United States during the last war although our losses
had been much less bitter. We cannot forget the hideous attitudes
toward loyal Americans of German descent.

Well do I remember that some days after the Armistice I announced that the food blockade against Germany should be removed
at once. That was imperative for reasons of humanity and for the
self-interest of the Allies that Bolshevism could be stopped in starving
Germany and that peace could be made. Despite these obvious reasons, the reaction in every part of the Allied world and the United
States was one of indignant opposition and denunciation of any mercy.
It took us months to secure so simple an act.

In the end from this furnace fire of hate statesmen are no longer
free agents. The bitterness makes sane peace almost impossible.
Those of us who observed the making of the Treaty of Versailles
knew that the leaders were consciously or unconsciously dominated
by the fires of hate still burning. They had to get their acts approved
at home. The sufferings of their people had been too great for rational action.

And one of the consequences of those hates was a treaty which
sowed the dragon's teeth of the present war.

In the present war the forces making for hate are even more violent. If this war continues long enough these hates will sit again at
the peace-table. Unless there be some allaying force, some entry of
reason and compassion, there will be a Carthaginian peace.

The conclusion of this observation is, "What powerful nation will still retain good will and reason?"

AND THE CAMP-FOLLOWER REVOLUTION

Hate, this sixth Horseman, continues to ride after so-called peace is made. Famine and Pestilence, together with the aftermaths of war's destruction, malnutrition, unemployment and poverty, furnish the fuel of class hate. It is hungry people who revolt in violence. Civilians with filled stomachs do not face machine-guns. Helpless, distraught, frustrated peoples accept the leadership of Hate, who mobilizes them into Revolution. The end is dictatorship and the advance Horsemen start on the march again.

AN AMERICAN ROLE

Now America has a role to perform. It can be a great role in our history.

There is no such thing as isolation for the United States from this war. The Monroe Doctrine itself is denial of that. And there can be no such thing as economic or intellectual or moral or spiritual isolation. There can be no isolation from world effort to allay misery, to save human life, to bring peace, disarmament, and reconstruction and renewed hope from this catastrophe. There can be isolation from military participation in this war. When I speak of joining in these wars I mean joining in the military side—sending our sons into it.

If we join in these wars we would start with the already great exhaustion of ten years of our depression. Then we will further exhaust our economic strength. And that exhaustion will be to a far greater degree than in the few months we participated in the last war. And when the war is over we shall need devote our remaining resources to support our wounded, our maimed, our orphaned and our destitute. We shall need every resource to rebuild our farmers and workers from our own misery and impoverishment. And our sympathies will be justly limited to suffering at home.

If we join in this war the last great remaining strength will have been exhausted. And hope of world recuperation will have been delayed while Revolution marches unimpeded over the earth.

If we join in this war we ourselves will develop all the hates that are inevitable from war. We shall have lost the voice of reason in the making of the peace.

And though we stay out, in our indignation at wrong and aggression we must not be led into blind hates against whole peoples. The great masses of the German people and the Russian people did not wish for the wars now going on. The vast majority of both these nations are gentle, decent people who prayed for peace even as did you and I.

And ours is a doubly difficult position. In our emotions we have a different scene from Europe fighting race against race. We have the heritage of every European race. Our war-hates are not alone against the enemy. They cruelly divide our own people, not alone for the war but long after.

But if we remain out of war, we might, if we have the will to do so, use our unimpaired resources, our courage, our moral strength to do mankind infinite service.

By that service we could allay the destruction of war, and the ravages of Famine and Pestilence. That service of compassion could go far to save civilization, and restore hope to men. Free of Hate we could exert an insistent voice of reason in the making of peace.

And if we are again called upon for service in reconstruction we have a right to demand that reason and hope sit at the peace-table. Reason and hope for the world call for the restoration of those nations who have lost their freedom.

. . . The future and the safety of our country and of our democracy are overwhelmingly involved in events far beyond our borders. . . . Let us say to the democracies: "We Americans are vitally concerned in your defense of freedom. We are putting forth our energies, our resources and our organizing powers to give you the strength to regain and maintain a free world."

—FRANKLIN D. ROOSEVELT, 1941.

I ADDRESS YOU, the Members of the Seventy-seventh Congress, at a moment unprecedented in the history of the Union. I use the word "unprecedented," because at no previous time has American security been as seriously threatened from without as it is today.

Since the permanent formation of our government under the Constitution, in 1789, most of the periods of crisis in our history have related to our domestic affairs. Fortunately, only one of these—the four year War between the States—ever threatened our national unity. Today, thank God, one hundred and thirty million Americans, in forty-eight States, have forgotten points of the compass in our national unity.

It is true that prior to 1914 the United States often had been disturbed by events in other Continents. We had even engaged in two wars with European nations and in a number of undeclared wars in the West Indies, in the Mediterranean and in the Pacific for the maintenance of American rights and for the principles of peaceful commerce. In no case, however, had a serious threat been raised against our national safety or our independence.

The Four Freedoms Address to the Congress, January 6, 1941. Samuel I. Rosenman, *The Public Papers and Addresses of Franklin D. Roosevelt.* Harper and Brothers, New York, 1950, vol. IX, pp. 663-672.

What I seek to convey is the historic truth that the United States as a Nation has at all times maintained opposition to any attempt to lock us in behind an ancient Chinese wall while the procession of civilization went past. Today, thinking of our children and their children, we oppose enforced isolation for ourselves or for any part of the Americas.

That determination of ours was proved, for example, during the quarter century of wars following the French Revolution.

While the Napoleonic struggles did threaten interests of the United States because of the French foothold in the West Indies and in Louisiana, and while we engaged in the War of 1812 to vindicate our right to peaceful trade, it is, nevertheless, clear that neither France nor Great Britain nor any other nation was aiming at domination of the whole world.

In like fashion from 1815 to 1914—99 years—no single war in Europe or in Asia constituted a real threat against our future or against the future of any other American nation.

Except in the Maximilian interlude in Mexico, no foreign power sought to establish itself in this Hemisphere; and the strength of the British fleet in the Atlantic has been a friendly strength. It is still a friendly strength.

Even when the World War broke out in 1914, it seemed to contain only small threat of danger to our own American future. But as time went on, the American people began to visualize what the downfall of democratic nations might mean to our own democracy.

We need not over-emphasize imperfections in the Peace of Versailles. We need not harp on failure of the democracies to deal with problems of world reconstruction. We should remember that the Peace of 1919 was far less unjust than the kind of "pacification" which began even before Munich, and which is being carried on under the new order of tyranny that seeks to spread over every continent today. The American people have unalterably set their faces against that tyranny.

Every realist knows that the democratic way of life is at this moment being directly assailed in every part of the world—assailed either by arms, or by secret spreading of poisonous propaganda by those who seek to destroy unity and promote discord in nations still at peace.

During sixteen months this assault has blotted out the whole pattern of democratic life in an appalling number of independent nations, great and small. The assailants are still on the march, threatening other nations, great and small.

Therefore, as your President, performing my constitutional duty to "give to the Congress information of the state of the Union," I find it necessary to report that the future and the safety of our country and of our democracy are overwhelmingly involved in events far beyond our borders.

Armed defense of democratic existence is now being gallantly waged in four continents. If that defense fails, all the population and all the resources of Europe, Asia, Africa and Australasia will be dominated by the conquerors. The total of those populations and their resources greatly exceeds the sum total of the population and resources of the whole of the Western Hemisphere—many times over.

In times like these it is immature—and incidentally untrue—for anybody to brag that an unprepared America, single-handed, and with one hand tied behind its back, can hold off the whole world.

No realistic American can expect from a dictator's peace international generosity, or return of true independence, or world disarmament, or freedom of expression, or freedom of religion—or even good business.

Such a peace would bring no security for us or for our neighbors. "Those, who would give up essential liberty to purchase a little temporary safety, deserve neither liberty nor safety". . . .

There is much loose talk of our immunity from immediate and direct invasion from across the seas. Obviously, as long as the British Navy retains its power, no such danger exists. Even if there were no British Navy, it is not probable that any enemy would be stupid enough to attack us by landing troops in the United States from across thousands of miles of ocean, until it had acquired strategic bases from which to operate.

But we learn much from the lessons of the past years in Europe—particularly the lesson of Norway, whose essential seaports were captured by treachery and surprise built up over a series of years.

The first phase of the invasion of this Hemisphere would not be the landing of regular troops. The necessary strategic points would be occupied by secret agents and their dupes—and great numbers of them are already here, and in Latin America.

As long as the aggressor nations maintain the offensive, they—not we—will choose the time and the place and the method of their attack.

That is why the future of all American Republics is today in serious danger.

That is why this Annual Message to the Congress is unique in our history.

That is why every member of the Executive Branch of the Government and every member of the Congress faces great responsibility —and great accountability.

The need of the moment is that our actions and our policy should be devoted primarily—almost exclusively—to meeting this foreign peril. For all our domestic problems are now a part of the great emergency.

Just as our national policy in internal affairs has been based upon a decent respect for the rights and dignity of all our fellowmen within our gates, so our national policy in foreign affairs has been based on a decent respect for the rights and dignity of all nations, large and small. And the justice of morality must and will win in the end.

Our national policy is this:

First, by an impressive expression of the public will and without regard to partisanship, we are committed to all-inclusive national defense.

Second, by an impressive expression of the public will and without regard to partisanship, we are committed to full support of all those resolute peoples, everywhere, who are resisting aggression and are thereby keeping war away from our Hemisphere. By this support, we express our determination that the democratic cause shall prevail; and we strengthen the defense and security of our own nation.

Third, by an impressive expression of the public will and without regard to partisanship we are committed to the proposition that principles of morality and considerations for our own security will never permit us to acquiesce in a peace dictated by aggressors and sponsored by appeasers. We know that enduring peace cannot be bought at the cost of other people's freedom. . . .

Therefore, the immediate need is a swift and driving increase in our armament production. . . .

New circumstances are constantly begetting new needs for our safety. I shall ask this Congress for greatly increased new appropriations and authorizations to carry on what we have begun.

I also ask this Congress for authority and for funds sufficient to manufacture additional munitions and war supplies of many kinds, to be turned over to those nations which are now in actual war with aggressor nations.

Our most useful and immediate role is to act as an arsenal for them as well as for ourselves. They do not need man power. They do need billions of dollars worth of the weapons of defense.

The time is near when they will not be able to pay for them in ready cash. We cannot, and will not, tell them they must surrender, merely because of present inability to pay for the weapons which we know they must have.

I do not recommend that we make them a loan of dollars with which to pay for these weapons—a loan to be repaid in dollars.

I recommend that we make it possible for those nations to continue to obtain war materials in the United States, fitting their orders into our own program. Nearly all of their matériel would, if the time ever came, be useful for our own defense.

Taking counsel of expert military and naval authorities, considering what is best for our own security, we are free to decide how much should be kept here and how much should be sent abroad to our friends who by their determined and heroic resistance are giving us time in which to make ready our own defense.

For what we send abroad, we shall be repaid, within a reasonable time following the close of hostilities, in similar materials, or, at our option, in other goods of many kinds which they can produce and which we need.

Let us say to the democracies: "We Americans are vitally concerned in your defense of freedom. We are putting forth our energies, our resources and our organizing powers to give you the strength to regain and maintain a free world. We shall send you, in ever-increasing numbers, ships, planes, tanks, guns. This is our purpose and our pledge."

In fulfillment of this purpose we will not be intimidated by the threats of dictators that they will regard as a breach of international law and as an act of war our aid to the democracies which dare to resist their aggression. Such aid is not an act of war, even if a dictator should unilaterally proclaim it so to be.

When the dictators are ready to make war upon us, they will not wait for an act of war on our part. They did not wait for Norway or Belgium or the Netherlands to commit an act of war.

Their only interest is in a new one-way international law, which lacks mutuality in its observance, and, therefore, becomes an instrument of oppression.

The happiness of future generations of Americans may well depend upon how effective and how immediate we can make our aid felt. No one can tell the exact character of the emergency situations that we may be called upon to meet. The Nation's hands must not be tied when the Nation's life is in danger.

We must all prepare to make the sacrifice that the emergency—as serious as war itself—demands. Whatever stands in the way of speed and efficiency in defense preparations must give way to the national need.

A free nation has the right to expect full cooperation from all groups. A free nation has the right to look to the leaders of business, of labor, and of agriculture to take the lead in stimulating effort, not among other groups but within their own groups.

The best way of dealing with the few slackers or trouble makers in our midst is, first, to shame them by patriotic example, and, if that fails, to use the sovereignty of government to save government.

As men do not live by bread alone, they do not fight by armaments alone. Those who man our defenses, and those behind them who build our defenses, must have the stamina and courage which come from an unshakeable belief in the manner of life which they are defending. The mighty action which we are calling for, cannot be based on a disregard for all things worth fighting for.

The Nation takes great satisfaction and much strength from the things which have been done to make its people conscious of their individual stake in the preservation of democratic life in America. Those things have toughened the fibre of our people, have renewed their faith and strengthened their devotion to the institutions we make ready to protect.

Certainly this is no time to stop thinking about the social and economic problems which are the root cause of the social revolution which is today a supreme factor in the world.

There is nothing mysterious about the foundations of a healthy and strong democracy. The basic things expected by our people of their political and economic systems are simple. They are:

Equality of opportunity for youth and for others.

Jobs for those who can work.

Security for those who need it.

The ending of special privilege for the few.

The preservation of civil liberties for all.

The enjoyment of the fruits of scientific progress in a wider and constantly rising standard of living.

These are the simple and basic things that must never be lost sight of in the turmoil and unbelievable complexity of our modern world. The inner and abiding strength of our economic and political systems is dependent upon the degree to which they fulfill these expectations. . . .

In the future days, which we seek to make secure, we look forward to a world founded upon four essential human freedoms.

The first is freedom of speech and expression—everywhere in the world.

The second is freedom of every person to worship God in his own way—everywhere in the world.

The third is freedom from want—which, translated into world terms, means economic understandings which will secure to every nation a healthy peace time life for its inhabitants—everywhere in the world.

The fourth is freedom from fear—which, translated into world terms, means a world-wide reduction of armaments to such a point and in such a thorough fashion that no nation will be in a position to commit an act of physical aggression against any neighbor—anywhere in the world.

That is no vision of a distant millennium. It is a definite basis for a kind of world attainable in our own time and generation. That kind of world is the very antithesis of the so-called new order of tyranny which the dictators seek to create with the crash of a bomb.

To that new order we oppose the greater conception—the moral order. A good society is able to face schemes of world domination and foreign revolutions alike without fear.

Since the beginning of our American history we have been engaged in change—in a perpetual peaceful revolution—a revolution which goes on steadily, quietly adjusting itself to changing conditions—without the concentration camp or the quick-lime in the ditch. The world order which we seek is the cooperation of free countries, working together in a friendly, civilized society.

This Nation has placed its destiny in the hands and heads and hearts of its millions of free men and women; and its faith in freedom under the guidance of God. Freedom means the supremacy of human rights everywhere. Our support goes to those who struggle to gain those rights or keep them. Our strength is in our unity of purpose.

To that high concept there can be no end save victory.

. . . We must wage a peace to attract the highest hearts and the most competent hands and brains.
—FRANKLIN D. ROOSEVELT, 1944.

*W*E NOW FACE the enormous and complex problems of building with our Allies a strong world structure of peace.

In doing that historic job we shall be standing before a mighty bar of judgment—the judgment of all those who have fought and died in this war—the judgment of generations yet unborn—the very judgment of God. . . .

Peace, no less than war, must offer a spirit of comradeship, a spirit of achievement, a spirit of unselfishness, and indomitable will to victory.

We have waged war against the wilderness—against the mountains and the rivers—against the droughts and the storms. We have waged war against ignorance—against oppression—against intolerance.

We have waged war against poverty—against disease.

We fought the Revolutionary War for the principle that all men are created equal—and in that war we pledged "our lives, our fortunes, and our sacred honor."

This war, which we are now fighting, has been an interruption in

Franklin D. Roosevelt, Speech in Boston, Mass., November 4, 1944. *Ibid.*, vol. XIII, pp. 405-406.

the story of our forward progress; but it has also opened a new chapter—a chapter which it is for us now living to begin.

At the end of this war this country will have the greatest material power of any nation in the world.

It will be a clean, shining America—richer than any other in skilled workers, engineers, farmers, businessmen, scientists.

It will be an America in which there is a genuine partnership between the farmer and the worker and the businessman—in which there are abundant jobs and an expanding economy of peace.

And around us we see an unfinished world—a world of awakened peoples struggling to set themselves on the path of civilization—people struggling everywhere to achieve a higher cultural and material standard of living.

I say we must wage the coming battle for America and for civilization on a scale worthy of the way we have unitedly waged the battles against tyranny and reaction and wage it through all the difficulties and disappointments that may ever clog the wheels of progress.

And I say we must wage it in association with the United Nations with whom we have stood and fought—with the association ever growing.

I say we must wage a peace to attract the highest hearts and the most competent hands and brains.

That, my friends, is the conception I have of the meaning of total victory.

And that conception is founded upon faith—faith in the unlimited destiny—the unconquerable spirit—of America.

PREAMBLE TO THE CHARTER OF
THE UNITED NATIONS ORGANIZATION

... Our respective Governments ... have agreed to the present Charter of the United Nations and do hereby establish an international organization to be known as the United Nations. 1945.

𝒲ᴇ ᴛʜᴇ ᴘᴇᴏᴘʟᴇs of the United Nations determined
  to save succeeding generations from the scourge of war, which twice in our lifetime has brought untold sorrow to mankind, and
  to reaffirm faith in fundamental human rights, in the dignity and worth of the human person, in the equal rights of men and women and of nations large and small, and
  to establish conditions under which justice and respect for the obligations arising from treaties and other sources of international law can be maintained, and
  to promote social progress and better standards of life in larger freedom,
and for these ends
  to practice tolerance and live together in peace with one another as good neighbors, and
  to unite our strength to maintain international peace and security, and
  to ensure, by the acceptance of principles and the institution of methods, that armed force shall not be used, save in the common interest, and

to employ international machinery for the promotion of the economic and social advancement of all peoples,
have resolved to combine our efforts to accomplish these aims.

Accordingly, our respective Governments, through representatives assembled in the city of San Francisco, who have exhibited their full powers found to be in good and due form, have agreed to the present Charter of the United Nations and do hereby establish an international organization to be known as the United Nations.

IX. Super-Power

At the end of World War II the ideals of the Declaration of Independence were enshrined in the U.N. Charter, and the United States, incomparably the greatest of powers, was not only imitated but widely looked to for aid and advice. Americans appeared to have attained the goal so long sought by those who taught activism and those who advocated preaching by example—the Americanization of the world.

But it soon became apparent that the triumph was not complete. In areas of Europe under its occupation, the Soviet government scorned democratic processes, using coercion to install and keep in power Communist regimes. Communist parties endeavored to subvert regimes that were democratic or at least paid lip-service to American principles.

This was a new situation. In the past, the United States had been concerned largely with extending the area in which these principles would hold sway; the issue had not been whether to do so but where and how. Now, however, the question was how to go about defending areas into which American ideas had already spread.

From both the far left and the far right came questions as to whether democracy's apparent gains were real. In different ways, both former Vice-President Henry A. Wallace and Senator Robert A. Taft argued against attempting to protect all of what was loosely *called the free world. The large majority of the public, however, went along with President Harry S. Truman in a series of bold pronouncements and measures committing the nation to activism on a scale that not even Wilson had envisioned—the Truman Doctrine, the Marshall Plan, the Berlin airlift, the North Atlantic Treaty, and intervention in Korea.*

HENRY WALLACE AND

HARRY S. TRUMAN ON

ISSUES WITH THE U.S.S.R.

We must recognize that the world has changed and that today there can be no "one world" unless the United States and Russia can find some way of living together. . . . It will be fruitless to continue to seek solutions for the many specific problems that face us in the making of the peace and in the establishment of an enduring international order without first achieving an atmosphere of mutual trust and confidence. —HENRY WALLACE, 1946.

I HAVE BEEN increasingly disturbed about the trend of international affairs since the end of the war, and I am even more troubled by the apparently growing feeling among the American people that another war is coming and the only way that we can head it off is to arm ourselves to the teeth. Yet all of past history indicates that an armaments race does not lead to peace but to war. The months just ahead may well be the crucial period which will decide whether the civilized world will go down in destruction after the five or ten years needed for several nations to arm themselves with atomic bombs.

Letter to President Harry S. Truman, July 23, 1946. *New Republic*, September 30, 1946, pp. 401-406.

Therefore I want to give you my views on how the present trend toward conflict might be averted. . . .

I am fully appreciative of the efforts that have been made and the patience that has been exercised by our various representatives who have carried on negotiations with the Russians during the last few years. I am conscious of the aggravations they have put up with and of the apparent inconsistencies on the part of Russian representatives. On the other hand, I feel these very difficulties make it necessary for some of us who, from the outside, are watching the course of events to voice our opinions. . . .

PUT YOURSELF IN RUSSIA'S PLACE

How do American actions since V-J Day appear to other nations? I mean by actions the concrete things like $13 billion for the War and Navy Departments, the Bikini tests of the atomic bomb and continued production of bombs, the plan to arm Latin America with our weapons, production of B-29's and planned production of B-36's, and the effort to secure air bases spread over half the globe from which the other half of the globe can be bombed. I cannot but feel that these actions must make it look to the rest of the world as if we were only paying lip-service to peace at the conference table. These facts rather make it appear either (1) that we are preparing ourselves to win the war which we regard as inevitable or (2) that we are trying to build up a predominance of force to intimidate the rest of mankind. How would it look to us if Russia had the atomic bomb and we did not, if Russia had 10,000-mile bombers and air bases within a thousand miles of our coast lines and we did not?

PROBLEMS OF AMERICAN-RUSSIAN RELATIONSHIPS

In general, there are two over-all points of view which can be taken in approaching the problem of the United States-Russian relations. The first is that it is not possible to get along with the Russians and therefore war is inevitable. The second is that war with Russia would bring catastrophe to all mankind, and therefore we must find a way of living in peace. It is clear that our own welfare as well as that of the entire world requires that we maintain the latter point of view. I am sure that this is also your opinion. . . .

We should try to get an honest answer to the question of what the factors are which cause Russia to distrust us, in addition to the question of what factors lead us to distrust Russia. I am not sure that we have as a nation or an administration found an adequate answer to either question, although we have recognized that both questions are of critical importance.

Our basic distrust of the Russians, which has been greatly intensified in recent months by the playing up of conflict in the press, stems from differences in political and economic organizations. For the first time in our history defeatists among us have raised the fear of another system as a successful rival to democracy and free enterprise in other countries and perhaps even our own. I am convinced that we can meet that challenge as we have in the past by demonstrating that economic abundance can be achieved without sacrificing personal, political and religious liberties. We cannot meet it, as Hitler tried to, by an anti-Comintern alliance.

It is perhaps too easy to forget that despite the deepseated differences in our culture and intensive anti-Russian propaganda of some twenty-five years' standing, the American people reversed their attitudes during the crisis of war. Today, under the pressure of seemingly insoluble international problems and continuing deadlocks, the tide of American public opinion is again turning against Russia. In this reaction lies one of the dangers to which this letter is addressed.

WHY RUSSIA DISTRUSTS THE WEST

I should list the factors which make for Russian distrust of the United States and of the Western world as follows: The first is Russian history, which we must take into account because it is the setting in which Russians see all actions and policies of the rest of the world. Russian history for over a thousand years has been a succession of attempts, often unsuccessful, to resist invasion and conquest—by the Mongols, the Turks, the Swedes, the Germans and the Poles. The scant thirty years of the existence of the Soviet government has in Russian eyes been a continuation of their historical struggle for national existence. The first four years of the new regime, from 1917 through 1921, were spent in resisting attempts at destruction by the Japanese, British and French, with some American assistance, and by the several White Russian armies encouraged and financed by the Western powers. Then, in 1941, the Soviet state was almost conquered by the Germans after a period during which the Western European powers had apparently acquiesced in the rearming of Germany in the belief that the Nazis would seek to expand eastward rather than westward. The Russians, therefore, obviously see themselves as fighting for their existence in a hostile world.

Second, it follows that to the Russians all of the defense and security measures of the Western powers seem to have an aggressive intent. Our actions to expand our military security system—such steps as extending the Monroe Doctrine to include the arming of the Western Hemisphere nations, our present monopoly of the atomic bomb, our interest in outlying bases and our general support of the British Empire—appear to them as going far beyond the requirements of defense. I think we might feel the same if the United States were the only capitalistic country in the world, and the principal socialistic countries were creating a level of armed strength far exceeding anything in their previous history. . . .

Finally, our resistance to her attempts to obtain warm-water ports and her own security system in the form of "friendly" neighboring states seems, from the Russian point of view, to clinch the case. After twenty-five years of isolation and after having achieved the status of a major power, Russia believes that she is entitled to recognition of her new status. Our interest in establishing democracy in Eastern Europe, where democracy by and large has never existed, seems to her an attempt to reëstablish the encirclement of unfriendly neighbors which was created after the last war and which might serve as a springboard of still another effort to destroy her.

WHAT WE SHOULD DO

If this analysis is correct, and there is ample evidence to support it, the action to improve the situation is clearly indicated. The fundamental objective of such action should be to allay any reasonable Russian grounds for fear, suspicions and distrust. We must recognize that the world has changed and that today there can be no "one world" unless the United States and Russia can find some way of living together. For example, most of us are firmly convinced of the soundness of our position when we suggest the internationalization and defortification of the Danube or of the Dardanelles, but we would be horrified and angered by any Russian counter-proposal that would involve also the internationalizing and disarming of Suez or Panama. We must recognize that to the Russians these seem to be identical situations.

We should ascertain from a fresh point of view what Russia believes to be essential to her own security as a prerequisite to the writing of the peace and to coöperation in the construction of a world order. We should be prepared to judge her requirements against the background of what we ourselves and the British have insisted upon as essential to our respective security. We should be prepared, even at the expense of risking epithets of appeasement, to agree to reasonable Russian guarantees of security. The progress made during June and July on the Italian and other treaties indicates that we can hope to arrive at understanding and agreement on this aspect of the problem.

We should not pursue further the question of the veto in connection with atomic energy, a question which is irrelevant and should never have been raised. We should be prepared to negotiate a treaty which will establish a definite sequence of events for the establishment of international control and development of atomic energy. This, I believe, is the most important single question, and the one on which the present trend is definitely toward deadlock rather than ultimate agreement.

We should make an effort to counteract the irrational fear of Russia which is being systematically built up in the American people by certain individuals and publications. The slogan that communism and capitalism, regimentation and democracy, cannot continue to exist in the same world is, from a historical point of view, pure propaganda. Several religious doctrines, all claiming to be the only true gospel and salvation, have existed side by side with a reasonable degree of tolerance for centuries. This country was for the first half of its national life a democratic island in a world dominated by absolutist governments.

We should not act as if we too felt that we were threatened in today's world. We are by far the most powerful nation in the world, the only Allied nation which came out of the war without devastation and much stronger than before the war. Any talk on our part about the need for strengthening our defense further is bound to appear hypocritical to other nations. . . .

SUMMARY

This proposal admittedly calls for a shift in some of our thinking about international matters. It is imperative that we make this shift. We have little time to lose. Our post-war actions have not yet been adjusted to the lessons to be gained from experience of Allied coöperation during the war and the facts of the atomic age.

It is certainly desirable that, as far as possible, we achieve unity on the home front with respect to our international relations; but unity on the basis of building up conflict abroad would prove to be not only unsound but disastrous. I think there is some reason to fear that in our earnest efforts to achieve bipartisan unity in this country we may have given way too much to isolationism masquerading as tough realism in international affairs.

The real test lies in the achievement of international unity. It will be fruitless to continue to seek solutions for the many specific problems that face us in the making of the peace and in the establishment of an enduring international order without first achieving an atmosphere of mutual trust and confidence. The task admittedly is not an easy one. There is no question, as the Secretary of State has indicated, that negotiations with the Russians are difficult because of cultural differences, their traditional isolationism and their insistence on a visible *quid pro quo* in all agreements. But the task is not an insuperable one if we take into account that to other nations our foreign policy consists not only of the principles that we advocate but of the actions we take. . . .

I think that progressive leadership along the lines suggested above would represent and best serve the interests of the large majority of our people, would reassert the forward-looking position of the Democratic Party in international affairs, and finally, would arrest the new trend toward isolationism and a disastrous atomic world war.

Our policy toward the Soviet Union is guided by the same principles which determine our policies toward all nations. We seek only to uphold the principles of international justice which have been embodied in the Charter of the United Nations.

—HARRY S. TRUMAN, 1947.

*P*ROGRESS IN REACHING our domestic goals is closely related to our conduct of foreign affairs. . . . What we do, or fail to do, at home

State of the Union Message, January 6, 1947. *Congressional Record,* 80th Congress, 1st session, pp. 123-125.

affects not only ourselves but millions throughout the world. If we are to fulfill our responsibilities to ourselves and to other peoples, we must make sure that the United States is sound economically, socially, and politically. Only then will be we able to help bring about the elements of peace in other countries—political stability, economic advancement, and social progress. . . .

During the long months of debate on [peace] treaties, we have made it clear to all nations that the United States will not consent to settlements at the expense of principles we regard as vital to a just and enduring peace. We have made it equally clear that we will not retreat to isolationism. Our policies will be the same during . . . forthcoming negotiations. . . .

The delay in arriving at the first peace settlements is due partly to the difficulty of reaching agreement with the Soviet Union on the terms of settlement. Whatever differences there may have been between us and the Soviet Union, however, should not be allowed to obscure the fact that the basic interests of both nations lie in the early making of a peace under which the peoples of all countries may return, as free men and women, to the essential tasks of production and reconstruction. The major concern of each of us should be the promotion of collective security, not the advancement of individual security.

Our policy toward the Soviet Union is guided by the same principles which determine our policies toward all nations. We seek only to uphold the principles of international justice which have been embodied in the Charter of the United Nations. . . .

ATOMIC ENERGY

The United States has taken the lead in the endeavor to put atomic energy under effective international control. We seek no monopoly for ourselves or for any group of nations. We ask only that there be safeguards sufficient to insure that no nation will be able to use this power for military purposes. So long as all governments are not agreed on means of international control of atomic energy, the shadow of fear will obscure the bright prospects for the peaceful use of this enormous power. . . .

MILITARY POLICY

In 1946 the Army and Navy completed the demobilization of their wartime forces. They are now maintaining the forces which we need for national defense and to fulfill our international obligations.

We live in a world in which strength on the part of peace-loving nations is still the greatest deterrent to aggression. World stability can be destroyed when nations with great responsibilities neglect to maintain the means of discharging those responsibilities.

This is an age when unforeseen attack could come with unprecedented speed. We must be strong enough to defeat, and thus to forestall, any such attack. In our steady progress toward a more rational world order, the need for large armed forces is progressively declining; but the stabilizing force of American military strength must not be weakened until our hopes are fully realized. When a system of collective security under the United Nations has been established, we shall be willing to lead in collective disarmament, but, until such a system becomes a reality, we must not again allow our weakness to invite attack. . . .

National security does not consist only of an army, a navy, and an air force. It rests on a much broader base. It depends on a sound economy of prices and wages, on a prosperous agriculture, on satisfied and productive workers, on a competitive private enterprise free from monopolistic repression, on continued industrial harmony and production, on civil liberties and human freedoms—on all the forces which create in our men and women a strong moral fiber and spiritual stamina.

But we have a higher duty and a greater responsibility than the attainment of national security. Our goal is collective security for all mankind.

If we can work in a spirit of understanding and mutual respect, we can fulfill this solemn obligation which rests upon us.

The spirit of the American people can set the course of world history. If we maintain and strengthen our cherished ideals, and if we share our great bounty with war-stricken people over the world, then the faith of our citizens in freedom and democracy will spread over the whole earth and free men everywhere will share our devotion to these ideals.

Let us have the will and the patience to do this job together.

May the Lord strengthen us in our faith.

May He give us wisdom to lead the peoples of the world in His ways of peace.

I believe that it must be the policy of the United States to support free peoples who are resisting attempted subjugation by armed minorities or by outside pressures.   HARRY S. TRUMAN, 1947.

ONE OF THE primary objectives of the foreign policy of the United States is the creation of conditions in which we and other nations will be able to work out a way of life free from coercion. This was a fundamental issue in the war with Germany and Japan. Our victory was won over countries which sought to impose their will, and their way of life, upon other nations.

To insure the peaceful development of nations, free from coercion, the United States has taken a leading part in establishing the United Nations. The United Nations is designed to make possible lasting freedom and independence for all its members. We shall not realize

Harry S. Truman, "The Truman Doctrine" Address to the Congress, March 12, 1947. *Congressional Record*, 80th Congress, 1st session, pp. 535-537.

our objectives, however, unless we are willing to help free peoples to maintain their free institutions and their national integrity against aggressive movements that seek to impose upon them totalitarian regimes. This is no more than a frank recognition that totalitarian regimes imposed upon free peoples, by direct or indirect aggression, undermine the foundations of international peace and hence the security of the United States.

The peoples of a number of countries of the world have recently had totalitarian regimes forced upon them against their will. The Government of the United States has made frequent protests against coercion and intimidation, in violation of the Yalta agreement, in Poland, Rumania, and Bulgaria. I must also state that in a number of other countries there have been similar developments.

At the present moment in world history nearly every nation must choose between alternative ways of life. The choice is too often not a free one.

One way of life is based upon the will of the majority, and is distinguished by free institutions, representative government, free elections, guaranties of individual liberty, freedom of speech and religion, and freedom from political oppression.

The second way of life is based upon the will of a minority forcibly imposed upon the majority. It relies upon terror and oppression, a controlled press and radio, fixed elections, and the suppression of personal freedoms.

I believe that it must be the policy of the United States to support free peoples who are resisting attempted subjugation by armed minorities or by outside pressures.

I believe that we must assist free peoples to work out their own destinies in their own way.

I believe that our help should be primarily through economic and financial aid which is essential to economic stability and orderly political processes.

The world is not static, and the *status quo* is not sacred. But we cannot allow changes in the *status quo* in violation of the Charter of the United Nations by such methods as coercion, or by such subterfuges as political infiltration. In helping free and independent nations to maintain their freedom, the United States will be giving effect to the principles of the Charter of the United Nations.

It is necessary only to glance at a map to realize that the survival and integrity of the Greek nation are of grave importance in a much wider situation. If Greece should fall under the control of an armed minority, the effect upon its neighbor, Turkey, would be immediate and serious. Confusion and disorder might well spread throughout the entire Middle East.

Moreover, the disappearance of Greece as an independent state would have a profound effect upon those countries in Europe whose peoples are struggling against great difficulties to maintain their freedoms and their independence while they repair the damages of war.

It would be an unspeakable tragedy if these countries, which have struggled so long against overwhelming odds, should lose that victory for which they sacrificed so much. Collapse of free institutions and loss of independence would be disastrous not only for them but for the world. Discouragement and possibly failure would quickly be the lot of neighboring peoples striving to maintain their freedom and independence.

Should we fail to aid Greece and Turkey in this fateful hour, the effect will be far-reaching to the West as well as to the East.

We must take immediate and resolute action.

I therefore ask the Congress to provide authority for assistance to Greece and Turkey in the amount of $400,000,000 for the period ending June 30, 1948. . . .

In addition to funds, I ask the Congress to authorize the detail of American civilian and military personnel to Greece and Turkey, at the request of those countries, to assist in the tasks of reconstruction, and for the purpose of supervising the use of such financial and material assistance as may be furnished. . . .

This is a serious course upon which we embark.

I would not recommend it except that the alternative is much more serious.

The United States contributed $341,000,000,000 toward winning World War II. This is an investment in world freedom and world peace.

The assistance that I am recommending for Greece and Turkey amounts to little more than one tenth of one percent of this investment. It is only common sense that we should safeguard this investment and make sure that it was not in vain.

The seeds of totalitarian regimes are nurtured by misery and want. They spread and grow in the evil soil of poverty and strife. They reach their full growth when the hope of a people for a better life has died.

We must keep that hope alive.

The free peoples of the world look to us for support in maintaining their freedoms.

If we falter in our leadership, we may endanger the peace of the world—and we shall surely endanger the welfare of our own Nation.

Great responsibilities have been placed upon us by the swift movement of events.

I am confident that the Congress will face these responsibilities squarely.

Sooner or later Truman's program of unconditional aid to anti-Soviet governments will unite the world against America and divide America against herself. —HENRY WALLACE, 1947.

WE ARE HERE tonight because we want peace.

We are here tonight because we mean to have peace.

Speech at Madison Square Garden, March 31, 1947. *Congressional Record,* 80th Congress, 1st session, appendix, pp. A1572-A1573.

We are here tonight to state that the Truman doctrine endangers peace.

We are here tonight to assert that peace requires Americans to reject that doctrine and reaffirm their faith in a strong United Nations.

Our soldiers did not win one war to fight another. Our workers and farmers toiled for freedom not for fear. Our dead did not bequeath to their children a legacy of death.

The world is hungry. The world cries out not for American tanks and guns to destroy more lives and leave more hunger, but for American plows and food to fulfill the promise of peace.

The world is afraid. The world cries out, not for an American crusade in the name of hatred and fear of communism, but for a world crusade in the name of the brotherhood of man.

All of America's history was consecrated to that ideal. It was tested and proved in a great civil war. Twice in this generation Americans have fought for a free humanity. Today we come to a turning in freedom's road. Today America is in danger of turning aside.

In the name of crisis the President asks America to help the governments of Greece and Turkey.

In the name of crisis America is asked to ignore the world tribunal of the United Nations and take upon herself the role of prosecutor, judge, jury—and sheriff—what a role!

In the name of crisis facts are withheld, time is denied, hysteria is whipped up. The Congress is asked to rush through a momentous decision as if great armies were already on the march. I hear no armies marching. I hear a world crying out for peace. . . .

The administration and its . . . supporters argue that we must intervene alone in Greece because the United Nations is too weak to act. I have not forgotten the appeasement of Hitler. I remember that every betrayal of world solidarity against Hitler by Daladier and Chamberlain was made in the name of the weakness of the League of

Nations. Let us not betray the future. Let the world not destroy the United Nations as it once destroyed the League. . . .

Let us do for the United Nations what needs to be done to carry out these tasks.

If the United Nations is untested, let us test it.

If the United Nations is weak, let us strengthen it.

No one pretends that the United Nations will meet all needs and solve all problems overnight.

Patience and toil will not give us the millennium, but they will help to make a more decent world than we have ever known.

If we reject this course, the United Nations will crumble and man's hope will perish. Sooner or later Truman's program of unconditional aid to anti-Soviet governments will unite the world against America and divide America against herself.

The Truman program must turn the world against America. At our command freedom, in whose name Americans have died, will become a catchword for reaction. Once we grant unconditional loans to the undemocratic Governments of Greece and Turkey, then, in the name of freedom, every Fascist dictator will know that he has credit in our bank. Today it is the Governments of Greece and Turkey. Tomorrow it may be Peron and Chiang Kai-shek. Our banks will give dollars; our arsenals will give weapons. When that is not enough our people will be asked to give their sons.

The Truman program must turn Americans against each other. It will threaten everything in America that is worth fighting for. Intolerance is aroused. Suspicion is engendered. Men of the highest integrity in public life are besmirched. . . .

Intolerance has an insatiable appetite. Whom will its inquisition condemn if this drive continues? Every American who reads the wrong books; every American who means liberty when he says liberty; every American who stands up for civil rights; every American who speaks out for one world. . . .

Hatred and violence abroad, hatred and fear at home will be the fruits of the Truman doctrine. A strong United Nations can bring peace. Which do we choose—for America must choose. The world waits for the American people.

Where are the millions who supported Roosevelt's ideals? Where are the inheritors of our great tradition? In weariness and confusion many Americans have abandoned political action. Now they must return. Their country needs them. Americans of all parties, all faiths, all creeds must now speak out in one great voice for peace and freedom.

America is our country. Because we love America, because we want American to be free and at peace in a world free and at peace, we say:

No imperialist adventures. Support the United Nations.

Millions to feed the hungry. Not one cent to arm tyranny.

Down with intolerance and bigotry. Back to the faith of our fathers.

Our deepest concern with European recovery ... is that it is essential to the maintenance of the civilization in which the American way of life is rooted. It is the only assurance of the continued independence and integrity of a group of nations who constitute a bulwark for the principles of freedom, justice and the dignity of the individual.

*—*HARRY S. TRUMAN, 1947.

A PRINCIPAL CONCERN of the people of the United States is the creation of conditions of enduring peace throughout the world. In company with other peace-loving nations, the United States is striving to insure that there will never be a World War III. In the words

State of the Union Message to Congress, December 19, 1947. *Congressional Record,* 80th Congress, 1st session, pp. 11749-11754.

of the Charter of the United Nations, we are "determined to save succeeding generations from the scourge of war."

We seek lasting peace in a world where freedom and justice are secure and where there is equal opportunity for the economic well-being of all peoples.

To this end, the United States played a leading role in the founding of the United Nations. We have supported that organization at all times to the best of our ability and we have advanced a number of proposals for increasing its effectiveness in maintaining the economic, social and moral foundations of peace.

We are working in the United Nations toward the limitation and control of armaments and, in a step without precedent or parallel, have offered to place our most powerful weapon under international control provided that other nations agree to effective and enforceable safeguards against its use for destructive purposes.

The United States, in the conviction that a prerequisite to peace in the future is the just settlement of past differences, has labored to obtain fair and workable treaties of peace for former enemy states so that they may resume their places in the family of nations.

The United States has taken the lead in worldwide efforts to promote industrial and agricultural reconstruction and a revival of world commerce, for we know that enduring peace must be based upon increased production and an expanding flow of goods and materials among nations for the benefit of all.

Since the surrender of the Axis powers, we have provided more than $15 billion, in the form of grants and loans, for aid to victims of the war, to prevent starvation, disease, and suffering; to aid in the restoration of transportation and communications; and to assist in rebuilding war-devastated economies. This assistance has averted stark tragedy and has aided progress toward recovery in many areas of the world.

In these and many other ways, the people of the United States have abundantly demonstrated their desire for world peace and the freedom and well-being of all nations.

We must now make a grave and significant decision relating to our further efforts to create the conditions of peace. We must decide whether or not we will complete the job of helping the free nations of Europe to recover from the devastation of the war. Our decision will determine in large part the future of the people of that continent. It will also determine in large part whether the free nations of the world can look forward with hope to a peaceful and prosperous future as independent states, or whether they must live in poverty and in fear of selfish totalitarian aggression.

It is of vital importance to the United States that European recovery be continued to ultimate success. The American tradition of extending a helping hand to people in distress, our concern for the building of a healthy world economy which can make possible ever-increasing standards of living for our people, and our overwhelming concern for the maintenance of a civilization of free men and free institutions, all combine to give us this great interest in European recovery.

The people of the United States have shown, by generous contributions since the end of hostilities, their great sympathy and concern for the many millions in Europe who underwent the trials of war and enemy occupation. Our sympathy is undiminished, but we know that we cannot give relief indefinitely, and so we seek practical measures which will eliminate Europe's need for further relief.

Considered in terms of our own economy, European recovery is essential. The last two decades have taught us the bitter lesson that no economy, not even one so strong as our own, can remain healthy and prosperous in a world of poverty and want. . . .

Our deepest concern with European recovery, however, is that it is essential to the maintenance of the civilization in which the American way of life is rooted. It is the only assurance of the continued independence and integrity of a group of nations who constitute a bulwark for the principles of freedom, justice and the dignity of the individual.

The economic plight in which Europe now finds itself has intensified a political struggle between those who wish to remain free men living under the rule of law and those who would use economic distress as a pretext for the establishment of a totalitarian state.

The next few years can determine whether the free countries of Europe will be able to preserve their heritage of freedom. If Europe fails to recover, the peoples of these countries might be driven to the philosophy of despair—the philosophy which contends that their basic wants can be met only by the surrender of their basic rights to totalitarian control.

Such a turn of events would constitute a shattering blow to peace and stability in the world. It might well compel us to modify our own economic system and to forego, for the sake of our own security, the enjoyment of many of our freedoms and privileges.

It is for these reasons that the United States has so vital an interest in strengthening the belief of the people of Europe that freedom from fear and want will be achieved under free and democratic governments. . . .

A successful European recovery program will depend upon two essentials. The first is that each nation separately and all the nations together should take vigorous action to help themselves. The second essential is that sufficient outside aid should be made available to provide the margin of victory for the recovery program. . . .

Most of the necessary outside aid, if it is to come at all, must come from the United States. It is a simple fact that we are the only nation with sufficient economic strength to bridge the temporary gap between minimum European needs and war-diminished European resources. . . .

I recommend that legislation providing for United States aid in support of the European recovery program authorize the appropriation of $17 billion from April 1, 1948, to June 30, 1952. Appropriation for the period from April 1, 1948, to June 30, 1949, should be made in time for the program to be put into effect by April 1, 1948. Appropriations for the later years should be considered subsequently by the Congress on an annual basis. . . .

It is my belief that United States support of the European recovery program will enable the free nations of Europe to devote their great energies to the reconstruction of their economies. On this depend the restoration of a decent standard of living for their peoples, the development of a sound world economy, and continued support for the ideals of individual liberty and justice.

In providing aid to Europe we must share more than goods and funds. We must give our moral support to those nations in their struggle to rekindle the fires of hope and strengthen the will of their peoples to overcome their adversities. We must develop a feeling of teamwork in our common cause of combating the suspicions, prejudices, and fabrications which undermine cooperative effort, both at home and abroad.

This joint undertaking of the United States and a group of European nations, in devotion to the principles of the Charter of the United Nations, is proof that free men can effectively join together to defend their free institutions against totalitarian pressures, and to promote better standards of life for all their peoples.

HARRY S. TRUMAN AND

ROBERT A. TAFT ON

THE NORTH ATLANTIC TREATY

Events of this century have taught us that we cannot achieve peace independently. The world has grown too small. . . . The security and welfare of each member of this community depend upon the security and welfare of all. —HARRY S. TRUMAN, 1949.

I TRANSMIT HEREWITH for the consideration of the Senate a copy of the North Atlantic Treaty. . . .

This treaty is an expression of the desire of the people of the United States for peace and security, for the continuing opportunity to live and work in freedom.

Events of this century have taught us that we cannot achieve peace independently. The world has grown too small. The oceans to our east and west no longer protect us from the reach of brutality and aggression.

We have also learned—learned in blood and conflict—that if we are to achieve peace we must work for peace.

This knowledge has made us determined to do everything we can to insure that peace is maintained. We have not arrived at this deci-

Message to the Senate, April 12, 1949. *Congressional Record*, 81st Congress, 1st session, pp. 43-54.

sion lightly, or without recognition of the effort it entails. But we cannot escape the great responsibility that goes with our great stature in the world. Every action of this Nation in recent years has demonstrated the overwhelming will of our people that the strength and influence of the United States shall be used in the cause of peace, justice, and freedom.

In this determination, our people wholeheartedly accepted the Charter of the United Nations in 1945. Since then, we have worked unceasingly to reach international agreement through the United Nations and to make the United Nations a more effective instrument for its mighty task.

In the last year we have embarked on a great cooperative enterprise with the free nations of Europe to restore the vitality of the European economy—so important to the prosperity and peace of our country and the world.

The North Atlantic Treaty is further evidence of our determination to work for a peaceful world. . . .

The 12 nations which have signed this treaty undertake to exercise their right of collective or individual self-defense against armed attack, in accordance with article 51 of the United Nations Charter, and subject to such measures as the Security Council may take to maintain and restore international peace and security. The treaty makes clear the determination of the people of the United States and of our neighbors in the North Atlantic community to do their utmost to maintain peace with justice and to take such action as they may deem necessary if the peace is broken.

The people of the North Atlantic community have seen solemn agreements, designed to assure peace and the rights of small nations, broken one by one and the people of those nations deprived of freedom by terror and oppression. They are resolved that their nations shall not, one by one, suffer the same fate.

The nations signing this treaty share a common heritage of democracy, individual liberty, and the rule of law. The American members of the North Atlantic community stem directly from the European members in tradition and in love of freedom. We have joined together in the progressive development of free institutions, and we have shared our moral and material strength in the present task of rebuilding from the devastation of war.

The security and welfare of each member of this community depend upon the security and welfare of all. None of us alone can achieve economic prosperity or military security. None of us alone can assure the continuance of freedom.

Together, our joint strength is of tremendous significance to the future of free men in every part of the world. For this treaty is clear evidence that differences in language and in economic and political systems are no real bar to the effective association of nations devoted to the great principles of human freedom and justice.

This treaty is only one step—although a long one—on the road to peace. No single action, no matter how significant, will achieve peace. We must continue to work patiently and carefully, advancing with practical, realistic steps in the light of circumstances and events as they occur, building the structure of peace soundly and solidly. . . .

This treaty, adopted to deal with a particular emergency today, is binding upon us for 20 years to cover all kinds of circumstances which cannot possibly be forseen. . . . It cannot be described otherwise than as a military alliance. . . . This treaty, therefore, means inevitably an armament race. . . . It necessarily divides the world into two armed camps. —ROBERT A. TAFT, 1949.

THE PURPOSE of American foreign policy, as I see it, is to maintain the freedom of the people of this country and, insofar as con-

Speech in the U. S. Senate, July 11, 1949. *Congressional Record,* 81st Congress, 1st session, pp. 9205-9210.

sistent with that purpose, to keep this country at peace. We are, of course, interested in the welfare of the rest of the world because we are a humane nation. Our huge economic aid, however, is based on the belief that a world which is prosperous and well off is less likely to engage in war than one in which there are great inequities in the economic condition of different people.

In the past, we have considered that the best method of preserving the peace and security of this country is the maintenance of American armed forces sufficient to defend us against attack, and a wise diplomatic policy which does not antagonize other nations. Those still are the main essentials to the maintenance of peace in the world of today.

But as the world shrinks in size, as new weapons are developed, as we inevitably become more involved in the affairs of other countries, it has become apparent that these weapons alone will not assure peace. And so we have committed ourselves to the principle of an association of sovereign nations banded together to preserve peace by preventing and punishing aggression. In the United Nations Charter we accepted the principle that we would go to war in association with other nations against a nation found by the Security Council to be an aggressor. That was a tremendous departure from our previous policy, but one which I have always urged and approved. . . . I believe that all nations must ultimately agree, if we are to have peace, to an international law defining the duties and obligations of such nations, particularly with reference to restraint from aggression and war. I believe that there should be international courts to determine whether nations are abiding by that law, and I believe that there should be a joint armed force to enforce that law and the decisions of that court. I believe that in the end, the public opinion of the world will come to support the principle that nations like individuals are bound by law, and will insist that any nation which violates the law be promptly subjected to the joint action of nations guided by a determination to enforce the laws of peace.

It is quite true that the United Nations Charter as drafted does not yet reach the ideals of international peace and justice which I have described, but it goes a long way in that direction. . . .

The Atlantic Treaty as drawn is certainly no improvement over the United Nations, nor can it by any stretch of the imagination be regarded as a perfection of or supplement to that Charter. From the point of view of an international organization, it is a step backward. . . .

What is the nature of that treaty?

It is obviously, and I do not think it can be questioned, a defensive military alliance between certain nations, the essence of which is an obligation under article 5 to go to war if necessary with any nation which attacks any one of the signers of the treaty. Such an attack may come from outsiders or it may come from one of the signers of the treaty itself. . . . Our obligation is self-executing upon the occurrence of an armed attack. . . .

I fully agree with the effective argument in favor of the pact made by the distinguished Senator from Michigan [Republican Arthur H. Vandenberg] because of its warning to the U.S.S.R. I think we should make it clear to the U.S.S.R. that if it attacks western Europe, it will be at war with us. . . .

I agree that if the Kaiser had known that England and the United States would be in the war, the First World War might never have begun. I agree that if Hitler had known the United States would be in the war, the Second World War might not have begun. I favor the extension of the Monroe Doctrine under present circumstances to western Europe.

It is said that the Atlantic Treaty is simply another Monroe Doctrine. I wish it were. That would be much more acceptable to me than the Atlantic pact, arms or no arms. Let me point out the vital differences. The Monroe Doctrine was a unilateral declaration. We were free to modify it or withdraw from it at any moment. This treaty, adopted to deal with a particular emergency today, is binding upon us for 20 years to cover all kinds of circumstances which cannot possibly be foreseen. The Monroe Doctrine left us free to determine the merits of each dispute which might arise and to judge the justice and the wisdom of war in the light of the circumstances at the time. The present treaty obligates us to go to war if certain facts occur. The Monroe Doctrine imposed no obligation whatever to assist any American Nation by giving it arms or even economic aid. We were free to fight the war in such a manner as we might determine, or not at all. This treaty imposes on us a continuous obligation for 20 years to give aid to all the other members of the pact, and, I believe, to give military aid to all the other members of the pact.

All kinds of circumstances may arise which will make our obligation most inconvenient. The government of one of these nations may be taken over by the Communist Party of that nation. The distinguished Senator from Michigan says that we are then released from our obligation, but I see no basis whatever for such a conclusion. If that were true of a Communist government, it might also be true of a Socialist government if we did not happen to approve of socialism at the time. Presumably, it could be true of a Fascist government, one similar, perhaps, to that existing in Spain . . ., and which is not very different from the dictatorship of Portugal, which is a member of the pact and which has not a truly democratic form of government.

I cannot find anything in this treaty which releases us because we do not happen to like the officials in charge of the member nations at the particular moment.

Obviously, any help we give one of these nations today may be used later for aggressive purposes, against Russia or its satellites, or neutrals, or members of the pact, or it may even be used against us when we try to fulfill our obligation to other members of the pact. Except for the warning conveyed to Soviet Russia, this treaty does not bear the slightest resemblance to the Monroe Doctrine. . . .

I have come reluctantly to the conclusion . . . that the arms program . . . must be considered an integral part of the Atlantic Treaty.

If that is the fact, we have a very different problem from the one which is urged upon us. . . .

First. With the arms in the pact it is even more clear that the pact is a military alliance, a treaty by which one nation undertakes to arm half the world against the other half, and in which all the pact members agree to go to war if one is attacked. It cannot be described otherwise than a military alliance. . . .

While this is not an offensive alliance, the line between defense and offense nowadays is indeed a shadowy one. The Maginot Line was the essence of pure defense. Today it is the target of ridicule. Every good defense includes elements of offense. . . . The result is that no matter how defensive an alliance may be, if it carries the obligation to arm it means the building up of competitive offensive armament. This treaty, therefore, means inevitably an armament race, and armament races in the past have led to war.

The United Nations looks perhaps vainly to the reduction of armaments. The Atlantic Pact proposes to increase them. . . .

Second. The pact standing by itself would clearly be a deterrent to war. If Russia knows that if it starts a war it will immediately find itself at war with the United States, it is much less likely to start a war. I see and believe in the full force of that argument. That is why I would favor the extension of the Monroe Doctrine to Europe. But if Russia sees itself ringed about gradually by so-called defensive arms, from Norway to Denmark to Turkey to Greece, it may form a different opinion. It may decide that the arming of western Europe, regardless of its present purpose, looks to an attack upon Russia. Its view may be unreasonable, and I think it is. But from the Russian standpoint it may not seem unreasonable. They may well decide that if war is the certain result, that war might better occur now rather than after the arming of Europe is completed. . . .

Third. The pact with the arms obligation, I believe, violates our obligations under the United Nations. . . . I do not claim that there is any direct violation of the Charter, but the Atlantic Pact moves in exactly the opposite direction from the purposes of the Charter and makes a farce of further efforts to secure international peace through law and justice. It necessarily divides the world into two armed camps. It may be said that the world is already so divided, but it cannot be said that by enforcing that division we are carrying out the spirit of the United Nations.

Fourth. The obligation to furnish arms is either a mere token obligation, or it is one of vast extent. I do not know enough about modern military equipment to make any estimate. I have heard that to provide 60 divisions, which is said to be the very minimum necessary and perhaps completely inadequate against Russian attack, would cost a total of $24,000,000,000. We are entering on a new lend-lease. The history of these obligations has been that once begun, they cannot be easily brought to an end. Furthermore if the Russian threat justifies arms for all of western Europe, surely it justifies similar arms for Nationalist China, for Indochina, for India, and ultimately for Japan; and in the Near East for Iran, for Syria, and for Iraq. There is no limit to the burden of such a program, or its dangerous implications. . . .

I do not mind saying now that once we enter into the pact, or do not enter into the pact, I am quite willing to consider providing arms for a particular nation to meet a particular emergency. I voted for the Greek and Turkish loans to provide arms. There may be other cases. I think today the providing of arms in support of Nationalist China, where war is actually going on, is something that I would approve, but that is a very different thing from building up a tremendous armament for 11 different nations, implying so far as I can see, the obligation to do the same thing in the rest of the world.

In any way the result will not come from the battle put up by the western European countries. The outcome will finally depend on the armed forces of America. Let us keep our forces strong. Let us use the money we have for armament in building up the American Army, the American Air Forces, and the American Navy. Let us keep our forces strong, and spend the money that is available for arms for those forces, because in the last analysis, we will win a war only if the United States wins the war, no matter how we assist other nations. They may be of assistance here and there. We cannot be certain that they will fight. We cannot be sure what their position may be at the time. We cannot be sure that Communists will not take control in those nations. . . .

We have chosen to give economic assistance. That assistance is given on the theory that the Russians do not contemplate aggressive war, but intend to fight their battle by propaganda and a production of chaotic economic conditions. I believe the undertaking of both types of assistance is beyond the economic capacity of the United States. I believe we will have to choose whether we give economic assistance or arms. The first, I believe, has contributed and will contribute to peace. The second, I think, will make war more likely.

Fifth. The justification for the arms aid rests on the necessity of defense against Russia, but remember that once these arms are provided, they are completely within the control of the nation receiving them. They are subject to the orders of those who, at the time, control the government of the country. Those governors may be Communists or Fascists, they may be peace-loving, or they may be aggressors. In future years, these arms may be used against us instead of on our side. If Russia should choose to go to war within the next year or two, they might easily be captured by the Russians and turned against us. We would be playing a dangerous game if we encouraged every country in Europe to arm itself to the teeth. Modern arms are not toys.

It is said that arms given to European countries cannot be used by them in dealing with their colonial possessions outside the scope of the pact, but surely anyone can see that all the armed forces possessed by any country are in one pool and that the bigger the pool is, the more easily they can find arms to undertake action which may be considered aggression in their colonies. . . .

It is quite true that the economic aid we are giving will be used to build up competition for ourselves, but after all that is in the interest of international trade and, in the long run, we can look after ourselves in that field. But the assistance we give here may be used to bring about the death of American boys and the destruction of American cities. . . .

Mr. President, since I feel that this pact is inextricably linked with the arms program, and since I believe that, so linked, the program is a threat to the welfare of the people of the United States, I shall vote against the treaty. . . . I cannot escape the logic of the situation as I see it, and therefore I cannot vote for a treaty which, in my opinion, will do far more to bring about a third world war than it will ever maintain the peace of the world.

. . . We must continue to share in the common defense of free nations against aggression. At the last session, this Congress laid the basis for this joint effort. We must now put into effect the common defense plans that are being worked out.
                                                        —HARRY S. TRUMAN, 1950.

I AM HAPPY to be able to report to you today that the state of the Union continues to be good. Our Republic continues to increase in the enjoyment of freedom within its borders, and to offer strength and encouragement to all those who love freedom throughout the world.

During the past year we have made notable progress in strengthening the foundations of peace and freedom, abroad and at home.

We have taken important steps in securing the North Atlantic community against aggression. We have continued our successful support of European recovery. . . .

Today, by the grace of God, we stand a free and prosperous nation with greater possibilities for the future than any people have ever had before.

State of the Union Message, January 4, 1950. *Congressional Record,* 81st Congress, 2nd session, pp. 61-64.

We are now, in this year of 1950, nearing the midpoint of the twentieth century.

The first half of this century will be known as the most turbulent and eventful period in recorded history. The swift pace of events promises to make the next 50 years decisive in the history of man on this planet.

The scientific and industrial revolution which began two centuries ago has, in the last 50 years, caught up the peoples of the globe in a common destiny. Two world-shattering wars have proved that no corner of the earth can be isolated from the affairs of mankind.

The human race has reached a turning point. Man has opened the secrets of nature and mastered new powers. If he uses them wisely, he can reach new heights of civilization. If he uses them foolishly, they may destroy him.

Man must create the moral and legal framework for the world which will insure that his new powers are used for good and not for evil. In shaping the outcome, the people of the United States will play a leading role.

Among all the great changes that have occurred in the last 50 years, none is more important than the change in the position of the United States in world affairs. Fifty years ago, we were a country devoted largely to our own internal affairs. Our industry was growing, and we had new interests in the Far East and in the Caribbean, but we were primarily concerned with the development of vast areas of our own continental territory.

Today, our population has doubled. Our national production has risen from about 50 billion dollars, in terms of today's prices, to the staggering figure of 255 billion dollars a year. We have a more productive economic system and a greater industrial potential than any other nation on the globe. Our standard of living is an inspiration for all other peoples. Even the slightest changes in our economic and social life have their effect on other countries all around the world.

Our tremendous strength has brought with it tremendous responsibilities. We have moved from the outer edge to the center of world affairs. Other nations look to us for a wise exercise of our economic and military strength, and for vigorous support of the ideals of representative government and a free society. We will not fail them.

Our objective in the world is peace. Our country has joined with others in the task of achieving peace. We know now that this is not an easy task, or a short one. But we are determined to see it through. Both of our great political parties are committed to working together —and I am sure they will continue to work together—to achieve this end. We are prepared to devote our energy and our resources to this task, because we know that our own security and the future of mankind are at stake.

Our success in working with other nations to achieve peace depends largely on what we do at home. We must preserve our national strength. Strength is not simply a matter of arms and force. It is a matter of economic growth, and social health, and vigorous institutions, public and private. We can achieve peace only if we maintain our productive energy, our democratic institutions, and our firm belief in individual freedom.

Our surest guide in the days that lie ahead will be the spirit in which this great Republic was founded. We must make our decisions in the conviction that all men are created equal, that they are equally entitled to life, liberty, and the pursuit of happiness, and that the duty of government is to serve these ends.

This country of ours has experienced many blessings, but none greater than its dedication to these principles. At every point in our history, these ideals have served to correct our failures and shortcomings, to spur us on to greater efforts, and to keep clearly before us the primary purpose of our existence as a nation. They have enshrined for us, as a principle of government, the moral imperative to do justice, and the divine command to men to love one another.

These principles give meaning to all that we do.

In foreign policy, they mean that we can never be tolerant of oppression or tyranny. They mean that we must throw our weight on the side of greater freedom and a better life for all peoples. These principles confirm us in carrying out the specific programs for peace which we have already begun.

We shall continue to give our wholehearted support to the United Nations. We believe that this organization can ultimately provide the framework of international law and morality without which mankind cannot survive. . . .

We are working toward the time when the United Nations will control weapons of mass destruction and will have the forces to preserve international law and order. While the world remains unsettled, however, and as long as our own security and the security of the free world require, we will maintain a strong and well-balanced defense organization. . . .

Under the principles of the United Nations Charter, we must continue to share in the common defense of free nations against aggression. At the last session, this Congress laid the basis for this joint effort. We now must put into effect the common defense plans that are being worked out.

We shall continue our efforts for world economic recovery, because world prosperity is the only sure foundation for permanent peace.

An expanding world economy requires the improvement of living standards and the development of resources in areas where human poverty and misery now prevail. Without such improvement, the recovery of Europe and the future of our own economy will not be secure. . . .

It is more essential now than ever, if the ideals of freedom and representative government are to prevail in these areas, and particularly in the Far East, that their people experience, in their own lives, the benefits of scientific and economic advances. This program will require the movement of large amounts of capital from the industrial nations, and particularly from the United States, to productive uses in the underdeveloped areas of the world. Recent world events make prompt action imperative.

This program is in the interest of all people—and it has nothing in common with either the old imperialism of the last century or the new imperialism of the Communists.

Our aim for a peaceful, democratic world of free peoples will be achieved in the long run, not by force of arms, but by an appeal to the minds and hearts of men. If the peace policy of the democratic nations is to be successful, they must demonstrate that the benefits of their way of life can be increased and extended to all nations and all races.

In the world today, we are confronted with the danger that the rising demand of people everywhere for freedom and a better life may be corrupted and betrayed by the false promises of communism. In its ruthless struggle for power, communism seizes upon our imperfections and takes advantage of the delays and setbacks which the democratic nations experience in their effort to secure a better life for their citizens. This challenge to us is more than a military challenge. It is a challenge to the honesty of our profession of the democratic faith; it is a challenge to the efficiency and stability of our economic system; it is a challenge to our willingness to work with other peoples for world peace and world prosperity.

For my part, I welcome the challenge. I believe that our country, at this crucial point in world history, will meet that challenge successfully. I believe that, in cooperation with the other free nations of the world, we shall extend the full benefits of the democratic way of life to millions who do not now enjoy them, and preserve mankind from dictatorship and tyranny.

I believe that we shall succeed in our struggle for peace, because I have seen the success we have had in our own country in following the principles of freedom. Over the last 50 years, the ideals of liberty and equal opportunity to which our Nation is dedicated have been increasingly realized in the lives of our people.

The ideal of equal opportunity no longer means simply the opportunity which a man has to advance beyond his fellows. Some of our citizens do achieve greater success than others as a reward for individual merit and effort, and this is as it should be. At the same time, our country must be more than a land of opportunity for a select few. It must be a land of opportunity for all of us. In such a land, all can grow and prosper together.

The simple truth that we can all go forward together is often questioned by selfish or shortsighted persons. It is strange that this is so, for this proposition is so clearly demonstrated by our national history. During the last 50 years, for example, our nation has grown enormously in material well-being. This growth has come about, not by concentrating the benefits of our progress in the hands of a few, but by increasing the wealth of the great body of our citizens. . . .

Increasing freedom from poverty and drudgery has given a fuller meaning to American life. Our people are better educated; we have more opportunities for travel anad recreation and enjoyment of the arts. We enjoy more personal liberty in the United States today than ever before.

If we can continue in the spirit of cooperative adventure which has marked the recent years of our progress, we can expect further scientific advances, further increases in our standard of living, and a still wider enjoyment of democratic freedom. . . .

As we move forward into the second half of the twentieth century, we must always bear in mind the central purpose of our national life. We do not seek material prosperity for ourselves because we love luxury; we do not aid other nations because we wish to increase our power. We have not devised programs for the security and well-being of our people because we are afraid or unwilling to take risks. This is not the meaning of our past history or our present course.

We work for a better life for all, so that all men may put to good use the great gifts with which they have been endowed by their Creator. We seek to establish those material conditions of life in which, without exception, men may live in dignity, perform useful work, serve their communities, and worship God as they see fit.

These may seem simple goals, but they are not little ones. They are worth a great deal more than all the empires and conquests of history. They are not to be achieved by military aggression or political fanaticism. They are to be achieved by humbler means—by hard work, by a spirit of self-restraint in our dealings with one another, and by a deep devotion to the principles of justice and equality.

It should make us truly thankful, as we look back to the beginnings of this country, that we have come so far along the road to a better life for all. It should make us humble to think, as we look ahead, how much farther we have to go to accomplish, at home and abroad, the objectives that were set out for us at the founding of this Nation.

As we approach the halfway mark in the twentieth century, we should ask for continued strength and guidance from that Almighty Power who has placed before us such great opportunities for the good of mankind in the years to come.

X.   Perspectives of the Sixties

By the end of the Korean conflict in 1953, bounds had apparently been set to the expansion of Communism. In the following decade, the only significant change in the global balance of power was the shift of Cuba into the Sino-Soviet camp, but, after a crisis in October, 1962, in which President John F. Kennedy successfully demanded withdrawal of Russian missiles and bombers, that island became more a lonely outpost than a base for further spread of Communist ideology and dominion.

The debates of the post-World War II years and the decades preceding died down. As was manifest in the oratory of Presidents Eisenhower and Kennedy and other public leaders, the dream of an Americanized world remained bright. At times, as in Secretary of State John Foster Dulles' utterances on "liberation" of Eastern Europe, one heard echoes of the older activism. Occasionally, as in Ambassador George F. Kennan's discussion of possible "disengagement," one heard faint suggestions of America's returning to a purely exemplary role. But to most Americans the two concepts no longer made sense separately. The United States seemed committed for all time to an active role in the world, endeavoring to preserve the largest possible area for democracy and, with discretion, to expand it; and, at the same time, equally committed to being an example not only of freedom but of prosperity. The obligations seemed mutually consistent and a choice between them no longer necessary or even feasible.

The old debates were over. Statesmen were groping toward a sense of what the new issues might be—what the great debates would turn upon in their children's time.

DWIGHT D. EISENHOWER AND

JOHN F. KENNEDY ON

THE AMERICAN OUTLOOK AT

MID-CENTURY

We annually spend on military security more than the net income of all United States corporations. This conjunction of an immense military establishment and a large arms industry is new in the American experience. . . . In the councils of government, we must guard against the acquisition of unwarranted influence, whether sought or unsought, by the military-industrial complex. The potential for the disastrous rise of misplaced power exists and will persist.

—DWIGHT D. EISENHOWER, 1961.

W E NOW STAND ten years past the midpoint of a century that has witnessed four major wars among great nations. Three of these involved our own country. Despite these holocausts America is today the strongest, the most influential and most productive nation in the world. Understandably proud of this pre-eminence, we yet realize that America's leadership and prestige depend, not merely upon our unmatched material progress, riches and military strength, but on

Farewell Address, January 17, 1961. *Public Papers of the Presidents of the United States: Dwight D. Eisenhower, 1960-1961.* Government Printing Office, 1961, pp. 1036-1040.

how we use our power in the interests of world peace and human betterment.

Throughout America's adventure in free government, our basic purposes have been to keep the peace; to foster progress in human achievement, and to enhance liberty, dignity and integrity among people and among nations. To strive for less would be unworthy of a free and religious people. Any failure traceable to arrogance, or our lack of comprehension or readiness to sacrifice would inflict upon us grievous hurt both at home and abroad.

Progress toward these noble goals is persistently threatened by the conflict now engulfing the world. It commands our whole attention, absorbs our very beings. We face a hostile ideology—global in scope, atheistic in character, ruthless in purpose, and insidious in method. Unhappily the danger it poses promises to be of indefinite duration. To meet it successfully, there is called for, not so much the emotional and transitory sacrifices of crisis, but rather those which enable us to carry forward steadily, surely, and without complaint the burdens of a prolonged and complex struggle—with liberty the stake. Only thus shall we remain, despite every provocation, on our charted course toward permanent peace and human betterment.

Crises there will continue to be. In meeting them, whether foreign or domestic, great or small, there is a recurring temptation to feel that some spectacular and costly action could become the miraculous solution to all current difficulties. A huge increase in newer elements of our defense; development of unrealistic programs to cure every ill in agriculture; a dramatic expansion in basic and applied research— these and many other possibilities, each possibly promising in itself, may be suggested as the only way to the road we wish to travel.

But each proposal must be weighed in the light of a broader consideration: the need to maintain balance in and among national programs—balance between the private and the public economy, balance between cost and hoped for advantage—balance between the clearly necessary and the comfortably desirable; balance between our essential requirements as a nation and the duties imposed by the nation upon the individual; balance between actions of the moment and the national welfare of the future. Good judgment seeks balance and progress; lack of it eventually finds imbalance and frustration.

The record of many decades stands as proof that our people and their government have, in the main, understood these truths and have responded to them well, in the face of stress and threat. But threats, new in kind or degree, constantly arise. I mention two only.

A vital element in keeping the peace is our military establishment. Our arms must be mighty, ready for instant action, so that no potential aggressor may be tempted to risk his own destruction.

Our military organization today bears little relation to that known by any of my predecessors in peacetime, or indeed by the fighting men of World War II or Korea.

Until the latest of our world conflicts, the United States had no armaments industry. American makers of plowshares could, with time and as required, make swords as well. But now we can no longer risk emergency improvisation of national defense; we have been compelled to create a permanent armaments industry of vast proportions. Added to this, three and a half million men and women are directly engaged in the defense establishment. We annually spend on military security more than the net income of all United States corporations.

This conjunction of an immense military establishment and a large arms industry is new in the American experience. The total influence —economic, political, even spiritual—is felt in every city, every State house, every office of the Federal government. We recognize the imperative need for this development. Yet we must not fail to comprehend its grave implications. Our toil, resources and livelihood are all involved; so is the very structure of our society.

In the councils of government, we must guard against the acquisition of unwarranted influence, whether sought or unsought, by the military-industrial complex. The potential for the disastrous rise of misplaced power exists and will persist.

We must never let the weight of this combination endanger our liberties or democratic processes. We should take nothing for granted.

Only an alert and knowledgeable citizenry can compel the proper meshing of the huge industrial and military machinery of defense with our peaceful methods and goals, so that security and liberty may prosper together.

Akin to, and largely responsible for, the sweeping changes in our industrial-military posture, has been the technological revolution during recent decades.

In this revolution, research has become central; it also becomes more formalized, complex, and costly. A steadily increasing share is conducted for, by, or at the direction of, the Federal government. . . .

The prospect of domination of the nation's scholars by Federal employment, project allocations, and the power of money is ever present —and is gravely to be regarded.

Yet, in holding scientific research and discovery in respect, as we should, we must also be alert to the equal and opposite danger that public policy could itself become the captive of a scientific-technological elite.

It is the task of statemanship to mold, to balance, and to integrate these and other forces, new and old, within the principles of our democratic system—ever aiming toward the supreme goals of our free society.

Another factor in maintaining balance involves the element of time. As we peer into society's future, we—you and I, and our government—must avoid the impulse to live only for today, plundering, for our own ease and convenience, the precious resources of tomorrow. We cannot mortgage the material assets of our grandchildren without risking the loss also of their political and spiritual heritage. We want democracy to survive for all generations to come, not to become the insolvent phantom of tomorrow.

Down the long lane of the history yet to be written America knows that this world of ours, ever growing smaller, must avoid becoming a community of dreadful fear and hate, and be, instead, a proud confederation of mutual trust and respect.

Such a confederation must be one of equals. The weakest must come to the conference table with the same confidence as do we, protected as we are by our moral, economic, and military strength. That table, though scarred by many past frustrations, cannot be abandoned for the certain agony of the battlefield. . . .

You and I—my fellow citizens—need to be strong in our faith that all nations, under God, will reach the goal of peace with justice. May we be ever unswerving in devotion to principle, confident but humble with power, diligent in pursuit of the Nation's great goals.

To all the peoples of the world, I once more give expression to America's prayerful and continuing aspiration:

We pray that peoples of all faiths, all races, all nations, may have their great human needs satisfied; that those now denied opportunity shall come to enjoy it to the full; that all who yearn for freedom may experience its spiritual blessings; that those who have freedom will understand, also, its heavy responsibilities; that all who are insensitive to the needs of others will learn charity; that the scourges of poverty, disease and ignorance will be made to disappear from the earth, and that, in the goodness of time, all peoples will come to live together in a peace guaranteed by the binding force of mutual respect and love.

Let every nation know, whether it wishes us well or ill, that we shall pay any price, bear any burden, meet any hardship, support any friend, oppose any foe to assure the survival and the success of liberty.
—JOHN F. KENNEDY, 1961.

W E OBSERVE today not a victory of party but a celebration of freedom, symbolizing an end as well as a beginning, signifying re-

Inaugural Address, January 20, 1961. *Public Papers of the Presidents: John F. Kennedy, 1961.* Government Printing Office, 1961, pp. 1-3.

newal as well as change. For I have sworn before you and Almighty God the same solemn oath our forebears prescribed nearly a century and three-quarters ago.

The world is very different now. For man holds in his mortal hands the power to abolish all forms of human poverty and all forms of human life. And yet the same revolutionary belief for which our forebears fought is still at issue around the globe, the belief that the rights of man come not from the generosity of the state but from the hand of God.

We dare not forget today that we are the heirs of that first revolution. Let the word go forth from this time and place, to friend and foe alike, that the torch has been passed to a new generation of Americans, born in this century, tempered by war, disciplined by a hard and bitter peace, proud of our ancient heritage, and unwilling to witness or permit the slow undoing of those human rights to which this nation has always been committed, and to which we are committed today at home and around the world.

Let every nation know, whether it wishes us well or ill, that we shall pay any price, bear any burden, meet any hardship, support any friend, oppose any foe to assure the survival and the success of liberty.

This much we pledge—and more.

To those old allies whose cultural and spiritual origins we share, we pledge the loyalty of faithful friends. United, there is little we cannot do in a host of cooperative ventures. Divided, there is little we can do, for we dare not meet a powerful challenge at odds and split asunder.

To those new states whom we welcome to the ranks of the free, we pledge our word that one form of colonial control shall not have passed away merely to be replaced by a far more iron tyranny. We shall not always expect to find them supporting our view. But we shall always hope to find them strongly supporting their own freedom, and to remember that, in the past, those who foolishly sought power by riding the back of the tiger ended up inside.

To those peoples in the huts and villages of half the globe struggling to break the bonds of mass misery, we pledge our best efforts to help them help themselves, for whatever period is required, not because the Communists may be doing it, not because we seek their votes, but because it is right. If a free society cannot help the many who are poor, it cannot save the few who are rich.

To our sister republics south of our border, we offer a special pledge: to convert our good words into good deeds, in a new alliance for progress, to assist free men and free governments in casting off the chains of poverty. But this peaceful revolution of hope cannot become the prey of hostile powers. Let all our neighbors know that we shall join with them to oppose aggression or subversion anywhere in the Americas. And let every other power know that this hemisphere intends to remain the master of its own house.

To that world assembly of sovereign states, the United Nations, our last best hope in an age where the instruments of war have far outpaced the instruments of peace, we renew our pledge of support: to prevent it from becoming merely a forum for invective, to strengthen its shield of the new and the weak, and to enlarge the area in which its writ may run.

Finally, to those nations who would make themselves our adversary, we offer not a pledge but a request: that both sides begin anew the quest for peace, before the dark powers of destruction unleashed by science engulf all humanity in planned or accidental self-destruction.

We dare not tempt them with weakness. For only when our arms are sufficient beyond doubt can we be certain beyond doubt that they will never be employed.

But neither can two great and powerful groups of nations take comfort from our present course—both sides overburdened by the cost of modern weapons, both rightly alarmed by the steady spread of the deadly atom, yet both racing to alter that uncertain balance of terror that stays the hand of mankind's final war.

So let us begin anew, remembering on both sides that civility is not a sign of weakness, and sincerity is always subject to proof. Let us never negotiate out of fear, but let us never fear to negotiate.

Let both sides explore what problems unite us instead of belaboring those problems which divide us.

Let both sides, for the first time, formulate serious and precise proposals for the inspection and control of arms, and bring the absolute power to destroy other nations under the absolute control of all nations.

Let both sides seek to invoke the wonders of science instead of its terrors. Together let us explore the stars, conquer the deserts, eradicate disease, tap the ocean depths and encourage the arts and commerce.

Let both sides unite to heed in all corners of the earth the command of Isaiah to "undo the heavy burdens . . . [and] let the oppressed go free."

And if a beachhead of cooperation may push back the jungle of suspicion, let both sides join in creating a new endeavor, not a new balance of power, but a new world of law, where the strong are just and the weak secure and the peace preserved.

All this will not be finished in the first one hundred days. Nor will it be finished in the first one thousand days, nor in the life of this Administration, nor even perhaps in our lifetime on this planet. But let us begin.

In your hands, my fellow citizens, more than mine, will rest the final success or failure of our course. Since this country was founded, each generation of Americans has been summoned to give testimony to its national loyalty. The graves of young Americans who answered the call to service surround the globe.

Now the trumpet summons us again—not as a call to bear arms, though arms we need; not as a call to battle, though embattled we are; but a call to bear the burden of a long twilight struggle, year in and year out, "rejoicing in hope, patient in tribulation," a struggle against the common enemies of man: tyranny, poverty, disease and war itself.

Can we forge against these enemies a grand and global alliance, North and South, East and West, that can assure a more fruitful life for all mankind? Will you join in that historic effort?

In the long history of the world, only a few generations have been granted the role of defending freedom in its hour of maximum danger. I do not shrink from this responsibility; I welcome it. I do not believe that any of us would exchange places with any other people or any other generation. The energy, the faith, the devotion which we bring to this endeavor will light our country and all who serve it, and the glow from that fire can truly light the world.

And so, my fellow Americans, ask not what your country can do for you; ask what you can do for your country.

My fellow citizens of the world, ask not what America will do for you, but what together we can do for the freedom of man.

Finally, whether you are citizens of America or citizens of the world, ask of us here the same high standards of strength and sacrifice which we ask of you. With a good conscience our only sure reward, with history the final judge of our deeds, let us go forth to lead the land we love, asking His blessing and His help, but knowing that here on earth God's work must truly be our own.

. . . We propose to complete the revolution of the Americas, to build a hemisphere where all men can hope for a suitable standard of living, and all can live out their lives in dignity and in freedom.
                              —JOHN F. KENNEDY, 1961.

*$\mathcal{F}$*OR THE FIRST TIME we have the capacity to strike off the remaining bonds of poverty and ignorance, to free our people for the

John F. Kennedy, *Alliance for Progress Address to Latin American diplomats*, March 19, 1961. *Ibid.*, pp. 170-175.

spiritual and intellectual fulfillment which has always been the goal of our civilization.

Yet at this very moment of maximum opportunity, we confront the same forces which have imperiled America throughout its history, the alien forces which once again seek to impose the despotisms of the old world on the people of the new. . . .

Our . . . task is to demonstrate to the entire world that man's unsatisfied aspiration for economic progress and social justice can best be achieved by free men working within a framework of democratic institutions. If we can do this in our own hemisphere, and for our own people, we may yet realize the prophecy of the great Mexican patriot, Benito Juarez, that "democracy is the destiny of future humanity." . . .

Therefore I have called on all the people of the hemisphere to join in a new Alliance for Progress—*Alianza para Progreso*—a vast cooperative effort, unparalleled in magnitude and nobility of purpose, to satisfy the basic needs of the American people for homes, work and land, health and schools—*techo, trabajo y tierra, salud y escuela.*

First, I propose that the American Republics begin on a vast new Ten-Year Plan for the Americas, a plan to transform the 1960's into an historic decade of democratic progress. . . .

Second, I will shortly request a ministerial meeting of the Inter-American Economic and Social Council, a meeting at which we can begin the massive planning effort which will be at the heart of the Alliance for Progress.

For if our Alliance is to succeed, each Latin nation must formulate long-range plans for its own development, plans which establish targets and priorities, insure monetary stability, establish the machinery for vital social change, stimulate private activity and initiative, and provide for a maximum national effort. These plans will be the foundation of our development effort, and the basis for the allocation of outside resources. . . .

Third, I have this evening signed a request to the Congress for $500 million as a first step in fulfilling the Act of Bogotá. This is the first large-scale inter-American effort, instituted by my predecessor President Eisenhower, to attack the social barriers which block economic progress. The money will be used to combat illiteracy, improve the productivity and use of the land, wipe out disease, attack archaic tax and land tenure structures, provide educational opportunities and offer a broad range of projects designed to make the benefits of increasing abundance available to all. . . .

Fourth, we must support all economic integration which is a genuine step toward larger markets and greater competitive opportunity. . . .

Fifth, the United States is ready to cooperate in serious, case-by-case examinations of commodity market problems. Frequent violent changes in commodity prices seriously injure the economies of many Latin-American countries, draining their resources, and stultifying their growth. . . .

Sixth, we will immediately step up our Food-for-Peace emergency program, help to establish food reserves in areas of recurrent drought, and help provide school lunches for children and offer feed grains for use in rural development. . . .

Seventh, all the people of the hemisphere must be allowed to share in the expanding wonders of science, wonders which have captured man's imagination, challenged the powers of his mind, and given him the tools for rapid progress. I invite Latin-American scientists to work with us in new projects in fields such as medicine and agriculture, physics and astronomy and desalinization; and to help plan for regional research laboratories in these and other fields; and to strengthen cooperation between American universities and laboratories. . . .

Eighth, we must rapidly expand the training of those needed to man the economies of rapidly developing countries. This means expanded technical training programs, for which the Peace Corps, for example, will be available when needed. It also means assistance to Latin-American universities, graduate schools and research institutes. . . .

Ninth, we reaffirm our pledge to come to the defense of any American nation whose independence is endangered. As its confidence in the collective security system of the Organization of American States spreads, it will be possible to devote to constructive use a major share of those resources now spent on the instruments of war. . . .

Tenth, we invite our friends in Latin America to contribute to the enrichment of life and culture in the United States. We need teachers of your literature and history and tradition, opportunities for our young people to study in your universities, access to your music, your art and the thought of your great philosophers. For we know we have much to learn. . . .

With steps such as these, we propose to complete the revolution of the Americas, to build a hemisphere where all men can hope for a suitable standard of living, and all can live out their lives in dignity and in freedom.

To achieve this goal political freedom must accompany material progress. Our Alliance for Progress is an alliance of free governments, and it must work to eliminate tyranny from a hemisphere in which it has no rightful place.

Therefore let us express our special friendship to the people of Cuba and the Dominican Republic, and the hope they will soon rejoin the society of free men, uniting with us in our common effort.

This political freedom must be accompanied by social change. For unless necessary social reforms, including land and tax reform, are freely made; unless we broaden the opportunity of all of our people; unless the great mass of Americans share in increasing prosperity, then our alliance, our revolution, our dream and our freedom will fail. But we call for social change by free men, change in the spirit of Washington and Jefferson, of Bolívar and San Martín and Martí, not change which seeks to impose on men tyrannies which we cast out a century and a half ago. Our motto is what it has always been: "Progress yes, tyranny no—*Progreso si, tirania no!*"

But our greatest challenge comes from within, the task of creating an American civilization where spiritual and cultural values are strengthened by an ever-broadening base of material advance, where, within the rich diversity of its own traditions, each nation is free to follow its own path toward progress.

The completion of our task will, of course, require the efforts of all the governments of our hemisphere. But the efforts of governments alone will never be enough. In the end, the people must choose and the people must help themselves.

And so I say to the men and women of the Americas—to the *campesino* in the fields, to the *obrero* in the cities, to the *estudiante* in the schools: prepare your mind and heart for the task ahead, call forth your strength and let each devote his energies to the betterment of all, so that your children and our children in this hemisphere can find an ever richer and a freer life. . . .

. . . We are well aware that all issues of principles are not settled, and that principles alone are not enough. It is therefore our intention to challenge the Soviet Union, not to an arms race, but to a peace race: to advance with us step by step, stage by stage, until general and complete disarmament has actually been achieved.

—JOHN F. KENNEDY, 1961.

𝒲E MEET in an hour of grief and challenge. Dag Hammarskjold is dead. But the United Nations lives on. His tragedy is deep in our hearts, but the task for which he died is at the top of our agenda. A noble servant of peace is gone. But the quest for peace lies before us.

The problem is not the death of one man; the problem is the life

John F. Kennedy, *Address on Disarmament* before the United Nations Assembly, September 25, 1961. *Ibid.*, pp. 618-626.

of this organization. It will either grow to meet the challenge of our age, or it will be gone with the wind, without influence, without force, without respect. Were we to let it die, to enfeeble its vigor, to cripple its power, we would condemn the future.

For in the development of this organization rests the only true alternative to war, and war appeals no longer as a rational alternative. Unconditional war can no longer lead to unconditional victory. It can no longer serve to settle disputes. It can no longer be of concern to great powers alone. For a nuclear disaster, spread by winds and waters and fear, could well engulf the great and the small, the rich and the poor, the committed and the uncommitted alike. Mankind must put an end to war or war will put an end to mankind.

So let us here resolve that Dag Hammarskjold did not live, or die, in vain. Let us call a truce to terror. Let us invoke the blessings of peace. And, as we build an international capacity to keep peace, let us join in dismantling the national capacity to wage war.

This will require new strength and new roles for the United Nations. For disarmament without checks is but a shadow, and a community without law is but a shell. Already the United Nations has become both the measure and the vehicle of man's most generous impulses. Already it has provided—in the Middle East, in Asia, in Africa this year in the Congo—a means to holding violence within bounds.

But the great question which confronted this body in 1945 is still before us: whether man's cherished hopes for progress and freedom are to be destroyed by terror and disruption; whether the "foul winds of war" can be tamed in time to free the cooling winds of reason; and whether the pledges of our Charter are to be fulfilled or defied: pledges to secure peace, progress, human rights and world law. . . .

Today, every inhabitant of this planet must contemplate the day when it may no longer be habitable. Every man, woman and child lives under a nuclear sword of Damocles, hanging by the slenderest of threads, capable of being cut at any moment by accident, miscalculation or madness. The weapons of war must be abolished before they abolish us.

Men no longer debate whether armaments are a symptom or cause of tension. The mere existence of modern weapons, ten million times more destructive than anything the world has ever seen, and only minutes away from any target on earth, is a source of horror and discord and distrust. Men no longer maintain that disarmament must await the settlement of all disputes, for disarmament must be a part of any permanent settlement. And men no longer pretend that the quest for disarmament is a sign of weakness, for in a spiraling arms race, a nation's security may well be shrinking even as its arms increase.

For fifteen years this organization has sought the reduction and destruction of arms. Now that goal is no longer a dream; it is a practical matter of life or death. The risks inherent in disarmament pale in comparison to the risks inherent in an unlimited arms race.

It is in this spirit that the recent Belgrade Conference, recognizing that this is no longer a Soviet problem or an American problem, but a human problem, endorsed a program of "general, complete and strictly an internationally controlled disarmament." It is in this same spirit that we in the United States have labored this year, with a new urgency, and with a new, now stautory agency fully endorsed by the Congress, to find an approach to disarmament which would be so far-reaching yet realistic, so mutually balanced and beneficial, that it could be accepted by every nation. And it is in this spirit that we have presented with the agreement of the Soviet Union, under the label both nations now accept of "general and complete disarmament," a new statement of newly agreed principles for negotiation.

But we are well aware that all issues of principles are not settled, and that principles alone are not enough. It is therefore our intention to challenge the Soviet Union, not to an arms race, but to a peace race: to advance with us step by step, stage by stage, until general and complete disarmament has actually been achieved. We invite them now to go beyond agreement in principle to reach agreement on actual plans.

The program to be presented to this Assembly, for general and complete disarmament under effective international control, moves to bridge the gap between those who insist on a gradual approach and those who talk only of the final and total achievement. It would create machinery to keep the peace as it destroys the machines of war. It would proceed through balanced and safeguarded stages designed to give no state a military advantage over another. It would place the final responsibility for verification and control where it belongs, not with the big powers alone, not with one's adversary or one's self, but in an international organization within the framework of the United Nations.

It would assure that indispensable condition of disarmament, true inspection, in stages proportionate to the stage of disarmament. It would cover delivery systems as well as weapons. It would ultimately halt their production as well as their testing, their transfer as well as their possession. It would achieve, under the eye of an international disarmament organization, a steady reduction in forces, both nuclear and conventional, until it had abolished all armies and all weapons except those needed for internal order and a new United Nations Peace Force. And it starts that process now, today, even as the talks begin.

In short, general and complete disarmament must no longer be a mere slogan, used to resist the first steps. It is no longer to be a goal without means of achieving it, without means of verifying its progress, without means of keeping the peace. It is now a realistic plan, and a test, a test of those only willing to talk and those willing to act.

Such a plan would not bring a world free from conflict or greed, but it would bring a world free from the terrors of mass destruction. It would not usher in the era of the super-state, but it would usher in an era in which no state could annihilate or be annihilated by another.

In 1945, this nation proposed the Baruch plan to internationalize the atom before other nations even possessed the bomb or demobilized their troops. We proposed with our allies the Disarmament Plan of 1951 while still at war in Korea. And we make our proposals today, while building up our defenses over Berlin, not because we are inconsistent or insincere or intimidated, but because we know the rights of free men will prevail, because while we are compelled against our will to rearm, we look confidently beyond Berlin to the kind of disarmed world we all prefer.

I therefore propose, on the basis of this plan, that disarmament negotiations resume promptly, and continue without interruption until an entire program for complete and general disarmament has not only been agreed upon but actually achieved.

The logical place to begin is a treaty assuring the end of nuclear tests of all kinds, in every environment, under workable controls. . . .

To destroy arms, however, is not enough. We must create even as we destroy, creating world-wide law and law enforcement as we outlaw world-wide war and weapons. In the world we seek, United Nations Emergency Forces which have been hastily assembled, uncertainly supplied and inadequately financed will never be enough.

Therefore, the United States recommends that all member nations earmark special peace-keeping units in their armed forces, to be on call to the United Nations, to be specially trained and quickly available, and with advance provision for financial and logistic support.

In addition, the American delegation will suggest a series of steps to improve the United Nations' machinery for the peaceful settlement of disputes, for on-the-spot fact-finding, mediation and adjudication, for extending the rule of international law. For peace is not solely a matter of military or technical problems; it is primarily a problem of politics and people. And unless man can match his strides in weaponry and technology with equal strides in social and political development, our great strength, like that of the dinosaur, will become incapable of proper control, and man, like the dinosaur, will vanish from the earth.

As we extend the rule of law on earth, so must we also extend it to man's new domain: outer space.

All of us salute the brave cosmonauts of the Soviet Union. The new horizons of outer space must not be riven by the old bitter concepts of imperialism and sovereign claims. The cold reaches of the universe must not become the new arena of an even colder war. . . .

But the mysteries of outer space must not divert our eyes or our energies from the harsh realities that face our own fellow men. Political sovereignty is but a mockery without the means to meet poverty and illiteracy and disease. Self-determination is but a slogan if the future holds no hope.

That is why my nation, which has freely shared its capital and its technology to help others help themselves, now proposes officially designating this decade of the 1960's as the United Nations Decade of Development. Under the framework of that resolution, the UN's existing efforts in promoting economic growth can be expanded and coordinated. Regional surveys and training institutes can pool the talents of many. New research, technical assistance and pilot projects can unlock the wealth of less-developed lands and untapped waters. And development can become a cooperative, not a competitive, enterprise, to enable all nations, however diverse in their systems and beliefs, to become in fact as well as law both free and equal states.

My country favors a world of free and equal states. We agree with those who say that colonialism is a key issue in this Assembly. But let the full facts of that be discussed in full.

On the one hand is the fact that, since the close of World War II, a world-wide declaration of independence has transformed nearly one billion people and nine million square miles into forty-two free and independent states. Less than 2 per cent of the world's population now lives in "dependent" territories.

I do not ignore the remaining problems of traditional colonialism which still confront this body. Those problems will be solved, with patience, good will and determination. Within the limits of our responsibility in such matters, my country intends to be a participant, not merely an observer, in the peaceful, expeditious movement of nations from the status of colonies to the partnership of equals. That continuing tide of self-determination has our sympathy and our support.

But colonialism in its harshest forms is not only the exploitation of new nations by old, of dark skins by light, or the subjugation of the poor by the rich. My nation was once a colony, and we know what colonialism means: the exploitation and subjugation of the weak by the powerful, of the many by the few, of the governed who have given no consent to be governed, whatever their continent, their class or their color.

And that is why there is no ignoring the fact that the tide of self-determination has not yet reached the Communist empire, where a population far larger than that officially termed "dependent" lives under governments installed by foreign troops instead of free institutions, under a system which knows only one party and one belief, which suppresses free debate, free elections, free newspapers, free books and free trade unions, and which builds a wall to keep truth a stranger and its own citizens prisoners. Let us debate colonialism in full, and apply the principle of free choice and the practice of free plebiscites in every corner of the globe. . . .

The events and decisions of the next ten months may well decide the fate of man for the next ten thousand years. There will be no avoiding these events. There will be no appeal from these decisions. And we shall be remembered either as the generation that turned this planet into a flaming funeral pyre or the generation that met its vow "to save succeeding generations from the scourge of war."

In the endeavor to meet that vow, I pledge you every effort this nation possesses. I pledge you that we shall neither commit nor provoke aggression, that we shall neither flee nor invoke the threat of force, that we shall never negotiate out of fear and we shall never fear to negotiate.

Terror is not a new weapon. Throughout history it has been used by those who could not prevail either by persuasion or by example. But inevitably they fail, either because men are not afraid to die for a life worth living or because the terrorists themselves come to realize that free men cannot be frightened by threats, and that aggression will meet its own response. And it is in the light of that history that every nation today should know, be he friend or foe, that the United States has both the will and the weapons to join free men in standing up to their responsibilities.

But I come here today to look across this world of threats to the world of peace. In that search we cannot expect any final triumph, for new problems will always arise. We cannot expect that all nations will adopt like systems, for conformity is the jailer of freedom, and the enemy of growth. Nor can we expect to reach our goal by contrivance, by fiat or even by the wishes of all.

But however close we sometimes seem to that dark and final abyss, let no man of peace and freedom despair. For he does not stand alone. If we all can persevere, if we can in every land and office look beyond our own shores and ambitions, then surely the age will dawn in which the strong are just and the weak secure and the peace preserved.

Ladies and gentlemen of this Assembly, the decision is ours. Never have the nations of the world had so much to lose or so much to gain. Together we shall save our planet or together we shall perish in its flames. Save it we can, and save it we must, and then shall we earn the eternal thanks of mankind and, as peacemakers, the eternal blessing of God.